Yogashaktı Shailaja Menon is a
is dedicated to spreading the wholesome message of
yoga in an accessible and understandable manner. Her
new book, Breathe, Bend, Be, is a classic example of her
amazing clarity of mind and purity of heart that shines
through each and every page. She has indeed distilled
the infinite wisdom of our ancient rishis and served it
in a palatable form to reach modern seekers. May this
monumental effort of hers transform thousands of lives
through the practice of dhyana, meditation that is indeed
the heart of yoga itself.

—Yogacharya Dr Ananda Balayogi Bhavanani
DSc (Yoga), Director, and Professor Yoga Therapy,
Institute of Salutogenesis and Complementary
Medicine (ISCM), Sri Balaji Vidyapeeth, Pondicherry,
India

* * *

Breathe, Bend, Be by Shailaja Menon offers a holistic
understanding of yoga and meditation in a simple and
effective manner to help achieve inner bliss, which also
alleviates mental health issues in the highly competitive
world in which we all live. She highlights how yoga
and meditation are inherently integral to each other,
through the exploration of Ashtanga yoga and offers easy
techniques to access higher levels of consciousness. The
writer truly inspires the readers to follow these practices

contd . . .

in their day-to-day lives by analysing them in a scientific manner.

Shailaja Menon's first book, *Yoga Shakti*, has contributed immensely to yoga literature with special emphasis on establishing the true meaning and intent of yoga. The second book in this series, *Breathe, Bend, Be,* provides much-needed nutrition for the mental awakening of the inner self through yogic practices.

—His Excellency B. N. Reddy
High Commissioner of India to Malaysia

* * *

Shailaja Menon's book, *Breathe, Bend, Be,* is a masterpiece, unfolding the ancient timeless wisdom of yoga into the practical application of Patanjali's eight limbs of yoga. Shailaja, through the lens of Ashtanga yoga, lays out for the seeker, the holistic path to higher consciousness. This book will help the reader to know themselves as they are. Meditation will then flower into a moment-to-moment awareness with the inner blossoming of bliss.

—Dr Vasant Lad
Ayurvedic Physician, Author, Educator, and Founder and Director, The Ayurvedic Institute, New Mexico

* * *

Shailaja Menon's new book offers clear directions for modern people to use ancient practices to assist them

contd . . .

in going beyond the limitations of their conditioning. It offers the freedom and equanimity that we all need to truly live meaningful, satisfying lives, which can be achieved by the step-by-step approach detailed herein.

—Dr Robert Svoboda
Ayurvedic Physician and Author

* * *

Shailaja Menon is known to me for over 20 years now, first as a journalist, and then as a yoga teacher and dear friend. Her teachings and writings have always come from a deep personal experience combined with the grace of her gurus. *Breathe, Bend, Be,* yet another expression of this inner evolution that Shailaja has embarked upon, will certainly connect the reader with some very deep concepts which can be practically applied in pursuit of one's own growth.

—Ramkumar
Vaidyagrama Ayurveda Healing Village, Coimbatore

* * *

In *Breathe, Bend, Be,* Shailaja Menon makes the complex and important topic of accessing higher states of consciousness like concentration and meditation accessible and understandable to everyone through the

contd . . .

eight limbs of yoga. The book takes the reader through traditional knowledge, contemporary research, and practical essentials. A definite guide on the journey within!

—Shirley Telles

MBBS, PhD, and Research Advisor, Patanjali Research Foundation, Haridwar

* * *

This book is one of the best I have read about yoga! It brings wisdom from ancient Indian scriptures like Patanjali Yoga Sutras and Bhagavad Gita and integrates it with brain research and modern writings from the Western yogis. This book is written in a simple and easy-to-read style and every chapter has practices that the reader can immediately try and experiment with. I highly recommend this book!

—Prasad Kaipa

PhD, Cofounder, Center for Consciousness Studies and Inner Transformation, Chairman, Samskrita Bharati USA, and Director, Yoga Bharati

* * *

What rishis heard in the deepest orders of meditation, is shruti and what they said afterwards are mantras and sutras. And one who interprets those sutras 'as it is' is a

contd . . .

credible teacher. Shailaja Menon is one of those credible teachers in our present times who is blessed with the ability to present difficult yogic concepts and techniques in a simple and effective way, without compromising its authenticity. Her book *Breathe, Bend, Be* is an amazing blend of conceptual clarity, practical exercises, scientific evidence, and scriptural references, which have been presented in a very understandable language. Certainly, a treat to the soul for readers.

—**Dr Vikrant Singh Tomar**
Global Convener United Consciousness, Founder-Director Project Self, USA/India, and Board member, European Yoga Federation

* * *

I only wish that Shailaja Menon could have published this book thirty years ago, when I began teaching yoga! Drawing from both East and West, the old and the new, the author uses the poetry of the Upanishads alongside Western research to unravel the mysteries of the mind and give hope and inspiration to those seeking to explore it.

A gifted writer, Shailaja maintains a conversational tone while she delves into profound and revelatory concepts, side by side with astute observations of contemporary life. Most of all, her love for yoga transmits through every page. This book will be a treasured manual for experienced students of yoga as well as for beginners.

— **Swami Divyananda Ma**

* * *

Shailaja Menon helped yoga seekers empower themselves through her fantastic first book *Yoga Shakti*. Now she aids us in mastering our minds by delving into the eight limbs of yoga. *Breathe, Bend, Be* indeed brings the ancient wisdom of the sages to the modern seekers in an easy and step-by-step manner. This book is a jewel and packs a punch delivering the much-needed precious teachings of Patanjali to help us have a better quality of life in today's challenging times. I strongly recommend everyone make this book a part of their wisdom library.

—**Kausthub Desikachar**
CEO and Chief Yoga Therapist, Viniyoga Internationa

BREATHE
BEND
BE

Exploring the Eight Limbs
of Yoga for Holistic Harmony

SHAILAJA MENON

HAY HOUSE INDIA
New Delhi • London • Sydney
Carlsbad, California • New York City

Hay House Publishers (India) Pvt Ltd
Muskaan Complex, Plot No. 3, B-2, Vasant Kunj, New Delhi – 110070, India

Hay House LLC, P.O. Box 5100, Carlsbad, CA 92018-5100, USA
Hay House UK Ltd, The Sixth Floor, Watson House, 54 Baker Street, London W1U 7BU, UK
Hay House Australia Publishing Pty Ltd, 18/36 Ralph St., Alexandria NSW 2015, Australia

Email: contact@hayhouse.co.in
Website: www.hayhouse.co.in

ISBN 978-81-19554-51-5
ISBN 978-81-19554-77-5 (ebook)

Dedication

To the late Padma Shri P. R. Krishna Kumar whose faith and vision in my path to share the ancient wisdom of yoga was far greater than anything I could conceive for myself. The energy and deep sense of purpose that exemplified his life continues to inspire and empower my life.

CONTENTS

Foreword I

Yoga, especially postures, breathing, and meditative practices, have earned a global cult status, cutting across boundaries of race, nationality, and religion. Adopted by millions, they are widely practised from the caves of the Himalayas to homes in Manhattan. Though the practice of yoga can be traced back 5,000 years, in the past few decades, with the spotlight on mental health, it has become more popular than ever.

One of the main reasons for its exponential growth is the body of evidence-based research that includes studies from prestigious institutions like Harvard, Stanford, Duke, and Oxford, to name a few, as well as leading research institutes in India that show the measurable benefits of breathing as well as meditation and mindfulness practices on brain and body. These studies have also shown the effectiveness of these practices when it comes to reversing neurodegeneration, reducing pain, managing stress, and dealing with a wide range of mental health issues including depression, anxiety and loneliness.

But even after such prominence and accessibility, yoga with its diverse traditions and practices can still be a daunting subject, especially for aspiring practitioners.

Breathe, Bend, Be breaks down the complex practice of yoga into a relatable and practical system. The book not only shares curated wisdom in a comprehensive format but also encourages the reader to participate and experience the transformative powers of yoga first-hand.

Shailaja, with her over two decades of passionate devotion to the field of yoga, first as a seeker and practitioner and then as a teacher, author, and speaker, brings to the book her wealth of personal knowledge, authenticity, and experientiality. She also provides an enlightening perspective on the practice of meditation as she explores in-depth the first six limbs of Ashtanga Yoga (eight limbs of yoga), part of the sacred scripture, the Yoga Sutras by Maharishi Patanjali, which leads to meditation. The different aspects of yoga are delved into and made to come alive as a vital entity essential for our evolution. Moreover, Shailaja brings her vibrancy and enthusiasm to each page and makes a strong case for the modern seeker to get started on the path.

All in all, *Breathe, Bend, Be* will help us harness and channelise the powers of our mind to actualise our goals. And as we connect to the realm of infinite potentiality that lies within each of us, where all possibilities exist, we may then go on to live the highest expression of ourselves.

I offer my best wishes to Shailaja and *Breathe, Bend, Be*, and that its much-needed message reaches genuine seekers far and wide across the globe and lights the spark of the inner quest.

— **R. Madhavan**
Actor, director, producer, and president of the
Film and Television Institute of India

Foreword II

Yoga is an age-old practice that continues to grow and spread its fragrance the world over. In today's challenging environment, stress management tools are the need of the hour. Mental health issues are on the rise globally and the advent of social media has also contributed to the increased incidence of problems like addiction, anxiety, depression, low self-worth and loneliness. In fact, though social media is touted as a tool of connection, it has in many cases, led to a deep sense of disconnection and isolation both in children and adults.

Thus, the practice of yoga helps a person to find the all-important connection with themselves and from that secure space interact with the world in a conscious and positive manner. They also reap the benefits of emotional and physical well-being by gaining an elevated perspective, and thus developing the capacity to consciously respond instead of instinctively reacting. All of these capacities translate into lower levels of stress and better parameters of health.

Shailaja Menon, in her book, *Breathe, Bend, Be,* based on Ashtanga yoga from the Yoga Sutras of Maharishi

Patanjali, has sought to explore the many layers of yoga so that the reader may gain a broader understanding of the different elements that go into navigating the terrains of the inner world. Through clear detailing of the different 'angas' of Ashtanga yoga over the many chapters, she lays down the inner work that is required for the reader to raise consciousness of their body, breath, mind, and energy. Every chapter also has practical exercises at the end so that reading the book is not just an intellectual exercise but an experiential one as well. Shailaja's desire to reach her readers and share her understanding in a manner that is beneficial to them shines through every page of the book.

I wish Shailaja and her book, *Breathe, Bend, Be*, great success. May it reach readers all over the world who seek authentic knowledge to elevate their minds and lives.

—K. K. Shailaja
Indian politician and
former Health Minister of Kerala

Preface

It's with great pride that I write this preface for my student Shailaja Menon, who has been learning all aspects of the practice and philosophy of yoga with me for the last twenty years.

The serene realms of the consciousness of the universe echo the wisdom of both manifestation and liberation. This timeless wisdom reverberates through the corridors of the interface of universal and individual human consciousness. This reverberation finds resonance and recognition in highly evolved beings called rishis. Yoga is one such gift of universal wisdom, poetically described as radiating from hiranya garbha or the splendorous womb. Patanjali is one of the great rishis who not only received yoga but in his compassion, scripted it out in what is now renowned as the *Yoga Sutras*.

The *Yoga Sutras* truly are a profound system of self-discovery—a path that can transcend us beyond the limitations of name, form, time, and space. The ashta angas constitutes one of the most sublime parts of the treatise of yoga sutras, and it is the wisdom of these 8 limbs that unfolds through the pages of this book. Every chapter will serve as a guide, a companion, and a whisperer of ancient truths in an accessible, practical way.

The journey begins with the Yamas and Niyamas, the precepts that form the foundation of this great practice. Within the pages that follow, Shailaja gently ushers the reader into the profound art of self-discipline, self-study, and surrender—the keys that unlock the gates to the boundless realm within.

In the labyrinth of modern existence, where chaos often reigns and the soul yearns for solace and freedom, Ashtanga yoga emerges as a sanctuary ... a sanctuary that beckons the seeker to return to the source, to rediscover the stillness within the ceaseless flux of life.

As you turn the pages of this book, envision it as the folds of a map that will guide you through the intricacies of the inner landscape. And, as you start applying the teachings of the book, they will serve as an alchemical process that transmutes the darkness of self-ignorance and suffering into crystalline self-realisation and joy.

This book is not a destination but a gateway to the boundless expanse of the human spirit. It is an invitation to delve into the wisdom of the ages and sip from the nectar of timeless teachings.

May this journey through *Breathe, Bend, Be* inspire you and embolden you to unravel the mysteries of your existence and discover the radiant light that has always resided within the sanctuary of your heart.

In reverence to the eternal flame of knowledge,

—Manoj Kaimal
Founder, Manasa Yoga

For Reader's Information

Maharishi Patanjali's teachings are based on Sankhya philosophy. Sankhya is a dwaitha philosophy where prakriti (nature) and purusha (consciousness) are separate. However, in the period post Adi Shankaracharya, the non-dual Advaita teachings gained wide acceptance. So, though this book is based on the eight limbs of yoga as given in the Yoga Sutras by Maharishi Patanjali, it also aligns with the Vedanta philosophy of Advaita (non-duality or oneness).

Kenesitam patati presitam manah kena pranah
prathamah praiti yuktah
kenesitam vacamimam vadanti caksuh srotram ka u
devo yunakti

(Willed by whom does the mind land upon its objects?
Willed by whom does the prana go in and out?
Willed by whom does speech originate? Which
effulgent being directs the eyes and ears?)

—Kenopanishad

Chapter 1

THE FUNDAMENTALS OF YOGA AND MEDITATION

The Origin of Yoga

Yoga is a journey to regain our universal nature which is described as sat-chit-ananda where sat means highest reality, chit means highest consciousness, and ananda translates to the highest bliss. To achieve this state, we need to move away from dvaitam (duality) which breeds separation, fear, and the survival instinct and move towards advaita, which is a state of oneness and integrated wholesomeness with the universe. In this state, we also experience sukham (ever-lasting peace and contentment). So, we can say that the process to get back to the state of oneness constitutes yoga practice.

According to Yogacharya Dr Ananda Balayogi Bhavanani, the history of yoga is timeless, and it is said that the origin of yoga can be tied to the origin of life itself. Also, there is evidence that shows that it originated in ancient India. The seals and fossil remains of the 5000-year-old Indus Saraswati Valley civilisation with motifs and figures in yogic postures reveal a fascinating story. One of the most well-known seals is the Pashupathi seal and it shows a man in mulabandhasana. This posture consists of sitting on top of your feet which are pointing backward. However, what is equally impressive is the representation of animals sitting calmly around the yogi Pashupati, who is also called the lord of animals. Some experts suggest that this is a metaphorical representation, and it indicates that through practising various postures, we can gain control over our bodies as well as our animalistic or impulsive minds.

Manoj Kaimal elaborates that when it comes to the mention of the word yoga, it is in the Rig Veda—an ancient and sacred scripture—that the word makes one of its earliest appearances. There it appears as part of a compound word yogakshema. The second half of the word, kshema, means that which confers happiness and auspiciousness. So, yoga, in that sense, was perhaps a practice for kshema. And this ideology still applies today. Whatever we do, if we can do it with the wisdom of yoga, a wholesomeness and beauty can be achieved in our every act.

The practice of yoga evolves us into more conscious beings. So, if we become aware that we slouch when we sit, we would consciously confer beauty to it by lifting our spine, drawing the chin back, opening the shoulders, and relaxing the face. Similarly, when we become aware of an unskillful pattern of thinking that drags us into anxiety and fear, we can consciously shift our attention to a more wholesome thought. This is referred to as kshema. Thus, the practice of yoga is not limited to what we do on a mat; it is an attitude, a philosophy, a wisdom-filled lens through which we view life. It is a way through which we lend auspiciousness, skillfulness, and beauty to life.

Who Is Maharishi Patanjali?

Yoga philosophy is one of the shad darshanas (six philosophical schools of Hinduism). And though yoga was being practised in the pre-Vedic period, it was the great sage Maharishi Patanjali who systemised and codified the then-existing practices of yoga, their meaning, and the related knowledge through his text, Yoga Sutras.

Maharishi Patanjali is often regarded as the father of yoga. He wrote the Yoga Sutras which consists of aphorisms about yoga, consciousness, and the human condition. But in the very first verse of the sutras, he clarifies his position.

The prefix anu in anushasanam denotes 'that which follows', thereby indicating that he is revealing now atha, a teaching tradition that existed before his time. Through atha and anu, Patanjali positions himself not as the originator but as an authority who undertakes the task of passing on the pre-existing yogic traditions to future generations of yoga practitioners. The 195 yoga sutras are terse verses pregnant with deep significance.

What Is Yoga?

A popular misconception is that yoga and asana are synonyms and are used interchangeably due to which in many parts of the world, they have come to mean the same thing. Contrary to this common belief, it is essential to recognise that yoga extends far beyond mere physical exercise. The ancient yogis did not engage in yoga practice to achieve flexible hamstrings, build a stronger core, or attain the aesthetically pleasing 'yoga butt' often depicted on social media.

In Patanjali's Ashtanga yoga system, yoga is a journey towards samyama, which encompasses dharana (concentration), dhyana (meditation), and samadhi (absorption). Also, Sage Vyasa, in his commentary on the Yoga Sutras, introduced the concept of the five chitta bhumis, or the five levels of consciousness. These states are experienced by all of us at various times, sometimes even within the same day, and we tend to fluctuate between them. These five states are: kshipta (restless), mudha (dull), vikshipta (intermittently focused), ekagra (one-pointed), and niruddha (dissolution). So essentially, yoga represents the journey of the mind, transitioning from a state of restlessness (kshipta) towards one-pointedness (ekagra) and ultimately dissolution (niruddha). The state of yoga can only be attained when the mind reaches the stages of ekagra and niruddha.

Thus, we can conclude that the practice of yoga focuses on cultivating qualities like concentration, attention, and absorption and the physical shapes and postures (asanas) we create with our bodies serve as valuable tools to aid us on this transformative path. While yoga may begin as a practice of stretching the body, it is, in essence, an ongoing and profound process of elevating the mind to access higher states of consciousness.

Need for Yoga

Today, yoga has become a well-known practice to relieve its practitioners from the tyranny of their minds and guide them towards states of health and wellness. We live in our minds and the state of our mind defines the state of our health and ultimately, our life. Thus, it is imperative, now more than ever, that we adopt these profound techniques to alleviate modern health issues like stress, anxiety, depression and insomnia.

Samadoshah samaagnishch samadhaatu malakriyah
Prasanna atmendriya manah swasth ityabhidheeyate.

(Health is a dynamic balance of the elements and humors, normal metabolic activity and efficient elimination coupled with a tranquil mind, senses and contented soul.)
— **Sushrut Samhita (15:41)**

Acharya Sushrut (~600 BC), an ancient Indian physician and surgeon, is generally referred to as the father of surgery. He had a profound perspective on health, defining it as 'a dynamic balance of the elements and humors, normal metabolic activity and efficient elimination coupled with a tranquil mind, senses and contented soul'. Additionally, the Yoga Vasistha, one of the great classical yoga texts attributed to Sage Valmiki and dating back over 5,000 years, already understood this psycho-somatic phenomenon with the term adhija-vyadhi. In the dialogue between the great sage Vasistha and Prince Rama, it describes disease (vyadhi) as a

manifestation of imbalances in the psyche (adhi) itself.
Yoga thus is the original mind-body medicine that has
the capacity to enable individuals to achieve a dynamic
state of wholesome health (swasth) at all levels of
existence—physical, mental, and spiritual.

Yogamaharishi Dr Swami Gitananda Giri also
echoed a similar sentiment. According to him, human
evolution is a journey from nara (disconnection with
self) to narayana (connection with the self), and the
reason we suffer at all levels of our existence—physical,
energetic, emotional, and spiritual—is because of this
disconnection. Other problems in life, be it loneliness,
anxiety, or depression also stem from these feelings
of isolation and disconnection. He elaborated this as
follows: 'The first disease is the sense of duality, leading
to fear that creates an imbalance of mind leading to
diseases in the body.' He further adds that yoga chikitsa
is the oldest holistic concept and therapy in the world
that assists in the return of the mind that feels separated
from the universe in which it exists.

The interconnection of mind, body, and breath isn't
merely just a yogic parlance; it's a profound understanding
that our ancient yogis unravelled thousands of years
ago through their extensive exploration of the human
body, psyche, and energy through asanas (postures),
pranayama (breathing techniques), and dhyana
(meditative practices). Today, modern science aligns
with this ancient wisdom.

Across the global medical community, it is well
established that chronic stress stands as a major
contributor to various illnesses. The primary reason for it

being that it weakens the immune system and interferes with the body's ability to regulate its inflammatory response. This, in turn, promotes the development and progression of many inflammatory diseases like cardiovascular disease, autoimmune diseases like rheumatoid arthritis, diabetes, inflammatory bowel disease, and neurodegenerative diseases like Alzheimer's, as well as certain types of cancer.

The encouraging news, supported by recent scientific research, is that the physiological, psychological, and biochemical impacts of yoga practice play a vital role in restoring autonomic balance. Yoga offers a path to relaxation, regeneration, and rejuvenation, impacting the human body across its various levels of existence.

What's the Purpose of Practising Yoga?

So, why do we engage in yoga practice? In the 2nd chapter of the Yoga Sutras, 'Sadhana Pada', Maharishi Patanjali provides a systematic framework for aspirants to alleviate suffering (dukha) through a methodical approach. However, before we embark on this journey, we must first recognise the existence of suffering. In sutra 2.15, he says, dukham eva sarvam vivekinah which translates to the wise one sees that all our pursuits end in suffering dukha, if we don't have discernment (viveka).

Patanjali's primary emphasis lies in the development of viveka, insightful discerning wisdom. As we cultivate the ability to delve deeper into the nature of dukha, which involves contemplative meditation, we gain insights into suffering being a result of false conjunction or 'samyoga'.

This means that we tend to superimpose identities onto various aspects of our lives. For instance, when we feel irritated, we attach it to an 'I', i.e., 'I am irritated'. Similarly, if our body gains weight, we identify with it and say, 'I am fat', and this leads to ongoing suffering. We also become deeply attached to objects, such as our car, job, position, relationships, and more. The stronger the identification, the more intense the suffering.

In essence, yoga practice aims to liberate the constant abduction of the 'I'. According to Maharishi Patanjali, this captivity is rooted in ignorance and is referred to as avidya. The path to liberation, as he clearly outlines in sutra 2.26, is through the attainment of wisdom, or prajna.

2.26 Vivekakhayatih aviplava hanopaya.

(The ceaseless flow of discriminative knowledge which guides thought, word and deed destroys ignorance, the source of pain.)

Another important question to consider here is how do we gain this discriminative wisdom (viveka)? It is here that Maharishi Patanjali gives us Ashtanga yoga.

2.28 Yoganganusthanat ashuddhiksaye jnanadiptir aviveka khyteh.

(By the dedicated practice of the various limbs of yoga, impurities are destroyed, and the lamp of knowledge starts to shine bright eventually becoming an all-purifying fire of viveka.)

And the next sutra, 2.29, elaborates on the eight limbs of Ashtanga yoga.

2.29 Yama niyama asana pranayama pratyahara dharana dhyana samadhayah astau angani.

(Moral codes [yama], ethical observances [niyama], postures [asana], regulation of breath [pranayama], withdrawal of senses [pratyahara], concentration [dharana], meditation [dhyana], absorption of consciousness in the self [samadhi] are the eight limbs of yoga.)

So, through the practice of the eight limbs of yoga, we move from suffering towards freedom, from suffering from the imprisonment of identity and a celebration of non-separateness.

What Is Meditation?

Meditation, a timeless practice deeply rooted in ancient Indian yogic texts, is a process that entails focusing and quieting the mind, allowing individuals to explore the depths of their consciousness and connect with the essence of their true selves. At its core, meditation involves a deliberate effort to shift one's awareness from the external world to the inner realm of thoughts, emotions, and sensations. This inner journey is guided by various techniques and methods that have been passed down through centuries, often based on the wisdom found in texts like *Yoga Sutras of Patanjali*, the Bhagavad Gita, and the Upanishads.

One fundamental aspect of meditation is the practice of concentration or dharana. This involves directing the mind's attention to a single point of focus, which can be an object, a sound, a mantra, or even the breath. By honing their concentration, practitioners learn to still the mental chatter and distractions that usually dominate their consciousness. Building upon concentration, meditation is the sustained and deepening state of focus. In this stage, the mind becomes increasingly tranquil and steady, paving the way for a profound inner journey. Ultimately, meditation leads to samadhi, the pinnacle of yogic practice. In this state, the practitioner transcends the boundaries of the individual self and merges with the universal consciousness. Samadhi is characterized by a profound sense of bliss, oneness, and transcendence of the ego.

An important point to note here is that meditation is not a passive endeavour; it requires discipline, patience, and committed practice. Ancient texts emphasise the importance of consistent effort and a dedicated spiritual journey. Over time, meditation enables individuals to gain self-awareness, access higher states of consciousness, and attain inner peace and wisdom. Moreover, meditation is not limited to sitting in a cross-legged posture; it can be practised in various forms, including mindfulness meditation, loving-kindness meditation, and mantra meditation, among others. Each approach offers a unique path to self-realisation and inner transformation.

In conclusion, meditation, deeply rooted in ancient Indian yogic traditions, is a transformative practice that involves concentration, deep focus, and ultimately transcending the limitations of the ego to achieve a profound state of unity and inner peace. It is a timeless journey of self-discovery and spiritual growth that continues to be practised by individuals seeking to explore the depths of their consciousness and connect with the universal source of wisdom and love.

Meditation Is a Skill

A reassuring fact is that meditation is a skill, and just like any other skill, it can be honed through dedication and perseverance. Consider how many times a baby falls before finding the balance to walk, or the countless attempts yoga practitioners make before achieving stability in challenging poses like handstands. Proficiency in any skill requires commitment, effort, and time, so it is crucial that we persevere and do not give up after a few initial, half-hearted attempts. The rewards it offers to our lives are profound and invaluable, making it a pursuit too significant to be approached or discarded casually.

Sri Swami Satchidananda shared his reflections on this subject as follows:

> And never think, 'Oh, I am unfit for meditation.' This is the biggest mistake many people make. They think that the minute they sit and close their eyes everything should be beautiful. If the mind runs here and there, they say, 'Meditation is not my thing.' It's like practising the piano or playing guitar or cooking. How many times have you cooked your fingers instead of vegetables? Nothing is learned that easily. While learning to bicycle how many times did you fall down? So, keep trying. Persevere.

One of the prerequisites of meditation is the cultivation of attention. According to philosopher William James, who wrote *The Principles of Psychology*, a groundbreaking text in the field of psychology, 'The faculty of bringing back a wandering attention over and over again is the very root of judgment, character and will.' He went on to add, 'An education which should improve this faculty would be the education, par excellence.'

It is crucial to emphasise that interest is a key ingredient for concentration to develop within us. We must genuinely enthuse ourselves to engage in the practice. Thus, it is essential to approach the practice with a keen awareness of its numerous benefits. These advantages encompass a profound transformation of our physical well-being, mental state, and overall life. They pave the way for us to unlock our highest potential, making them an unparalleled source of inspiration.

Are Yoga and Meditation Separate Practices?

With over two decades of experience as both a yoga practitioner and teacher, I have encountered several misconceptions regarding yoga, and one common fallacy is the perceived separation of yoga and meditation, as if they are unrelated practices. The foundation of this book draws from the Ashtanga yoga system outlined by Maharishi Patanjali in his Yoga Sutras. In the second chapter of these sutras, Maharishi Patanjali elucidates the path to samadhi, which he terms 'Ashtanga yoga', where 'ashta' signifies eight and 'anga' denotes limbs or facets. Within this systematically laid out path, meditation, or dhyana, is positioned as the seventh limb. Therefore, meditation isn't an isolated or independent practice; it is an integral component within the comprehensive framework of yoga.

In essence, yoga and meditation are not disparate practices; instead, they are intertwined facets of a holistic journey towards heightened awareness and self-realisation. This journey initiates with the awareness of the physical self, eventually expanding to encompass the profound depths of the mind, breath, and the interconnectedness of all aspects of existence. Through this alignment, individuals can uncover their unique purpose and, in harmony with the universe, express their highest potential. As Dr Ananda says in *Understanding the Yoga Darshan*, 'All of it is yoga. Yoga is everything and everything is yoga.'

In conclusion, we have explored the foundational principles of yoga including meditation and have dispelled some common misconceptions surrounding them. We have also discovered that these practices don't exist in isolation and instead, are inseparable, interconnected components within the path to self-awareness and spiritual evolution.

In the next chapter, we will see how science converges with these ancient disciplines, unravelling the scientific underpinnings that validate the transformative power of yoga and shedding light on the remarkable potential for healing, well-being, and spiritual awakening that these practices offer in our modern world.

* * *

Practical Exercise

Where Is the Mind?

- Throughout the day, periodically ask yourself this question. Doing so enhances your mindfulness regarding your mind's activities, its wanderings, and whether it gets stuck in repetitive thoughts in specific situations. This practice deepens your awareness and provides insights into your mind's workings. You can employ a timer initially, setting it for every 4 hours while you are awake, to prompt you to redirect your attention to your mind and pose this question. Much like the ancient yogis, who were early pioneers in studying the mind and its nature, we too should adopt this scientific approach.
- What is the emotional state of your mind? After locating your mind, the next step is to assess its emotional tone. Is it sad, happy, restless, sleepy, excited, frustrated, or angry? There is no judgement here. Your mind doesn't have to be happy all the time. The aim is simply to observe the mind, gaining insights into its functioning by directing your attention to it. Over time, this practice leads to a better understanding of yourself and a deeper connection with your own mind.

You can repeat this practice multiple times during the day to observe how your mind responds in various situations and to different people.

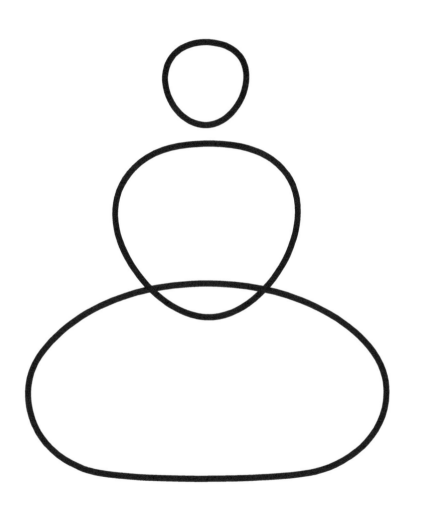

Srotrasya srotram manaso mano yad vaco ha
vacam sa u pranasya pranah
caksusacaksuratimucya dhirah
pretyasmallokadamrta bhavanti.

(It is indeed the self that is the ear of the ear, the
mind of the mind,
the speech of the speech, the prana of the prana
and the eye of the eye.)

—Kenopanishad

Chapter 2

Scientific Foundations of Yoga

The numerous health advantages of meditation are well-documented now. The book, *The Science of Meditation,* by Daniel Goleman & Richard J. Davidson elucidates that for long-term meditators, who have done about 1,000 hours or more of practice, there are brain and hormonal indicators of lowered reactivity to stress and lessened inflammation, a strengthening of the prefrontal circuits for managing distress, and lower levels of the stress hormones cortisol, signaling less reactivity to stresses in general.

Let's explore in depth the role of breathing practices and meditation when it comes to physical, mental, and social well-being.

Mind-Body Continuum

In the field of yoga, it is well-understood that mind and body are seamlessly connected. In other words, the mental state has a direct correlation with the state of the body. For instance, in moments of fear, the body tends to tense up; during shock, it may freeze, and in times of hopelessness, it can collapse. In fact, every thought we have has a corresponding effect on every cell in our body.

So, when we are stressed, hormones like cortisol, adrenalin, and epinephrine flood our bloodstream, affecting the heart, digestive system, and immune system. This reaction, known as the fight-or-flight response, activates the body by increasing heart rate, speeding up the breath, and sending blood to muscles that need to run. And we know that even though stress is experienced in the mind, it manifests in the body! In short, our psychology translates into our biology. Therefore, we can conclude mind and body are not separate.

According to the American Psychological Association in 2023, chronic stress affects all systems of the body including the musculoskeletal, respiratory, cardiovascular, endocrine, gastrointestinal, nervous and reproductive systems. It is also linked to some of the leading causes of illness and death including heart disease, cancer, lung ailments, accidents, cirrhosis of the liver, metabolic disorders like diabetes and obesity, immune disorders, infertility, substance abuse, depression, panic attacks, suicide, etc. The statistics may vary slightly but it is believed that 75 to 90 per cent of all doctors' visits are for stress-related ailments and complaints.

Meditation and Our Brain

Though once we believed that the brain was a static entity and wouldn't change over time, research in neuroscience has shown that the brain is dynamic, i.e., it is constantly wiring and rewiring itself and changing with every experience and thought. Neurons or nerve cells are constantly connecting and reconnecting to each other to form vast and intricate neural networks. Neurogenesis, the growth of new neurons, and synaptogenesis, the formation of new connections between existing neurons, are now linked to meditation. The brain's ongoing reshaping through repeated experiences, known as neuroplasticity, occurs continuously throughout the day. In other words, with our everyday thoughts and actions, our neurons are strengthening or weakening relevant brain circuitry and this knowledge puts the responsibility of nurturing and nourishing our brains firmly into our own hands!

According to Deepak Chopra in his book, *Super Brain*, 'Neuroplasticity is better than mind over matter. Its mind turning into matter as your thoughts create new neural growth.' Thus, we know now that we have the ability to consciously build happy, healthy brains which results in a healthy body as there is bidirectional communication between body and brain. At a neurochemical level, through our meditation practice, our body and brain are flooded by feel-good hormones like dopamine and serotonin, and this feel-good factor invites us to continue to return to the practice day after day.

With regular meditation practice, the corpus callosum—the thin white strip that connects the left and right hemispheres of the brain—gets stronger and thicker. Why is this so important? The corpus callosum is literally the bridge that helps communication flow between the left and the right brain; the critical and creative, the quantitative and qualitative aspects of the brain. When both the left and right hemispheres of the brain are harmonised, we have increased focus, deeper thought, more creativity, optimised mental health, better memory, and mental clarity.

In her first study, Neuroscientist Sara Lazar, from Mass General and Harvard Medical School, conducted medical tests on long-term meditators (those with seven to nine years of experience) and a control group consisting of people who didn't have any linkage with meditation. The results showed that those with a strong meditation background had increased grey matter in several areas of the brain, including the auditory and sensory cortex, as well as the insula and sensory regions. Not only that, but the results also showed that people who practised meditation had more grey matter in the frontal cortex, which is the part of the brain linked to decision-making and working memory. While most people's cortex shrink as they age, 50-year-old meditators in the study had the same amount of grey matter as those half their age.

Lazar and her team wanted to make sure that this wasn't because long-term meditators had more grey matter to begin with. So, in a second study, Lazar and her team put people with no experience with meditation into an 8-week mindfulness program. The results showed that just eight weeks of meditation changed people's brains for the better. There was thickening in several regions of the brain, including the left hippocampus (involved in learning, memory and emotional regulation), the TPJ (involved in empathy and the ability to take multiple perspectives), and a part of the brainstem called the pons (where regulatory neurotransmitters are generated). Plus, the brains of new meditators saw shrinkage of the amygdala, a region of the brain associated with fear, anxiety, and aggression. This reduction in the amygdala correlated to reduced stress levels in participants.

In these studies, participants were told to meditate for 40 minutes a day, but the average ended up being 27 minutes a day. Several other studies suggest that you can see significant positive changes in just 15 to 20 minutes a day. Thus, we can see that even a small amount of time dedicated to meditation can bring about significant changes.

Meditation and Gene Expression

We were always told that genes control our lives and that we are in effect the victims of our heredity. But through the science of epigenetics, we now know that it is the environment and our perception of the environment that triggers gene expression. Both positive and negative thoughts control our biology, so this knowledge again puts the responsibility squarely in our own hands to create a beautiful environment in our bodies and cells to manifest wellness and health.

Study leader, Ivana Buric, from the Centre for Psychology at Coventry University in the United Kingdom, and her colleagues found that mind-body interventions (MBIs) can reverse changes in our DNA that cause stress. The researchers recently reported their findings in 2017 in the journal *Frontiers in Immunology*. The team reviewed eighteen studies that had investigated the effects of numerous MBIs—including yoga, Tai Chi, meditation, and mindfulness—on gene expression. The studies included a total of 846 participants, who were followed up for an average of 11 years. From their analysis, the researchers found that people who practise MBIs experience reduced production of a molecule called nuclear factor kappa B (NF-kB), which is known to regulate gene expression.

The researchers explain that stressful events trigger activity in the sympathetic nervous system (SNS), which is responsible for the fight-or-flight response. This SNS activity leads to the production of NF-kB, which produces molecules called cytokines that promote cellular inflammation. If this molecular reaction is persistent, it can lead to serious physical and mental health problems, such as depression and even cancer. The study suggests that MBIs, however, lower the production of NF-kB and cytokines. This not only helps to alleviate stress, but it also helps to stave off the associated health conditions.

'Millions of people around the world already enjoy the health benefits of mind-body interventions like yoga or meditation, but what they perhaps don't realise is that these benefits begin at a molecular level and can change the way our genetic code goes about its business,' says Buric. 'These activities are leaving what we call a molecular signature in our cells, which reverses the effect that stress or anxiety would have on the body by changing how our genes are expressed. Put simply, MBIs cause the brain to steer our DNA processes along a path which improves our well-being.'

Yoga and the Autonomic Nervous System

The autonomic nervous system is the branch of the nervous system that carries out the vital functions of the heart, lungs, circulatory system, and glandular system without conscious intervention. It is further divided into sympathetic and parasympathetic. The sympathetic mediates the body's response to physical activity by increasing heart rate, blood pressure, muscle tone in the large skeletal muscles, sweat secretion, pupil dilation, and other functions. In short, it helps the body gear up for physical exertion. The parasympathetic does the opposite. It decreases heart rate, blood pressure, and skeletal muscle tone, preparing the body for rest, sleep, or digestion. Stimulation of one of these branches occurs involuntarily through various activities including eating, sleeping, exercising, and our mental processes. Additionally, every cycle of our breath also contributes to this stimulation. Inhalation emphasises sympathetic activity while exhalation stimulates parasympathetic activity. By adjusting the inhalation and exhalation through our pranayama practice, we can adjust the relative emphasis given to sympathetic or parasympathetic activities in each breath cycle to bring about balance in the body, mind, and energy level.

A conscious, slow, and long exhalation stimulates the vagus nerve, the 10th cranial nerve, which is the longest and most complex of the 12 pairs of cranial nerves that emanate from the brain. It is the body's weapon to counteract the flight-or-fight stress response. The term 'vagus' is derived from Latin, meaning 'wandering'. This name is apt as the vagus nerve meanders, much like a wanderer, throughout the body, connecting many vital organs from the brain stem to the colon. These organs include the heart, lungs, and abdomen, forming a communication pathway between these organs and the brain. The vagus nerve continuously monitors our breathing patterns and relays relevant messages to both the brain and heart. Additionally, it facilitates the transmission of information between the brain's surface and various tissues and organs throughout the body.

Therefore, when we engage in slow, deep, and focused breathing with emphasis on long exhalations, we activate the parasympathetic nervous system and induce the relaxation response in our bodies. This, in turn, leads to long-term improvements in mood, pain management, overall well-being, and resilience. Stimulation of the vagus nerve triggers the release of hormones such as serotonin, dopamine, and endorphins, which have a soothing effect on the nervous system, shifting it towards a state of rest and digestion. Additionally, it promotes the release of acetylcholine (Ach), a neurotransmitter that directly signals the heart to slow down. This reduction in heart rate is calming and signifies a decrease in the arousal level of the sympathetic nervous system. Practising slow inhalation and even slower exhalation increases heart rate variability, which measures the variation in heart rate between a breath in (when it naturally speeds up) and a breath out (when it naturally slows down). Higher heart rate variability is associated with lower chronic stress levels, better overall health, and enhanced cognitive function.

Healing Environment

Meditation is now being acknowledged as another important factor in the quest for good health along with diet, sleep, and exercise. Every day, we lose billions of cells through malnutrition, ageing, and damage, and we need to replace these cells. Also, when we are under stress, we shut down the growth and maintenance of the body as well as the immune system. So, if stress is sustained over a period of time, it will inevitably lead to disease and death. And though, our cells are constantly regenerating and the systems in our body are continually adapting to the surrounding circumstances and environment, there is only so much it can do. This is where meditation plays a vital role. Meditation creates the environment that activates the healing mechanism of our bodies which allows for the cells to repair and rejuvenate. Let's explore this further.

When we are stressed, our body releases adrenaline and cortisol. These chemicals are acidic and when they flood our body, it too becomes acidic, which, in turn, causes inflammation. This inflammation can lead to many chronic diseases including auto-immune diseases. But when we meditate, our body is flooded with dopamine, serotonin, and oxytocin, which are alkaline in nature. So, through a regular meditation practice, we are in effect changing the pH of the body. Serotonin is also responsible for maintaining mood balance and is commonly used in many antidepressants available today.

Beat Aging: The Telomeres Factor

Built into every one of our cells is the fountain of youth called telomeres. Telomeres are the caps at the end of each strand of DNA that protects our chromosomes, like the plastic tips at the end of our shoelaces. It protects the internal regions of the chromosomes and prevents their fusion with neighbouring chromosomes. Each time a cell divides, the telomeres get shorter. And just like how shoelaces become frayed when the plastic coating wears off, when the DNA runs out of telomeres, the cells can no longer do their jobs and ageing, disease, and depression set in. Due to this telomere length is closely correlated to cellular ageing, i.e., as we age the telomeres in our cells grow shorter.

Scientist Elizebeth Blackburn, who won the Noble Prize in 2009 in Physiology or Medicine, jointly with Carol W. Greider and Jack W. Szostak, noticed that the ends of the DNA with the telomeres had an enzyme telomerase and that it adds extensions to the telomeres. So, if the enzyme is working, the telomere can get longer and longer. And what would be the benefit of increasing the length of the telomere? In short, it would allow cells to keep on dividing without running out of DNA.

Some factors that contribute to the poor production of telomerase include poor nutrition, physical, verbal, and sexual abuse, post-traumatic stress disorder, loss of love or no self-love, and lack of purpose in life. These factors inhibit the telomerase enzymes from working as we subconsciously don't desire to live longer under these circumstances. This can be observed in the fact that a lot of people show a more rapid deterioration in their health after retirement because they lose their sense of purpose and service.

On the other hand, studies have shown that a healthy and holistic lifestyle boosts telomerase, which includes good nutrition, exercise, nurturing qualities such as happiness, gratitude, self-love, companionship, being in service as well as regularly practising yoga and meditation. In a study conducted in 2013, by Dr Dean Ornish from the Preventive Medicine Research Institute in Sausalito, California, 10 men in their early 60's were asked to follow a strict healthy living regime. They ate a meat-free diet, exercised for 30 minutes a day, did an hour of yoga and meditation a day, and attended group therapy sessions each week.

After five years, the telomeres on a type of white blood cell were on average 10 per cent longer in these men than at the start of the study. In contrast, 25 men who kept to their usual lifestyles saw telomeres on the same cells shrink by an average of 3 per cent over the same period. So, in a biological sense, these men actually got younger.

Mental Health

Over recent years, mental health has slowly moved out of the shadows and been gaining the attention it deserves. According to a March 2023 report from the World Health Organization, the global prevalence of depression has reached a staggering 280 million individuals. Alarmingly, depression is a significant factor contributing to suicide, which claims the lives of over 700,000 people annually. It is notably the fourth leading cause of death among individuals aged 15 to 29.

In a WHO Special Initiative for Mental Health Report spanning from 2019 to 2023, Devora Kestel, the director of the Department of Mental Health and Substance Abuse, revealed a startling statistic. She indicated that nearly one billion people worldwide are grappling with diagnosable mental health conditions. Moreover, it is estimated that the ongoing pandemic has led to a concerning 25 to 27 per cent increase in the prevalence of depression and anxiety across the globe. These figures show that tools to manage stress, including breathing practices and meditation, are the need of the hour.

Respond Versus React

When we are stressed, our bodies involuntarily react to the flight-or-fight mechanism. Though we know better than to scream at our kids or parents, we just react in accordance with the baseline level of stress in our nervous system. When anger or anxiety is triggered, the amygdala, which is part of the limbic system and plays a central role in our emotional responses, hijacks and paralyses the executive function of the brain (prefrontal cortex), and we react instead from a place of fear and stress (amygdala). Through regular meditation practice, we strengthen our capacity to consciously direct our attention, strengthen the prefrontal cortex, and quieten the amygdala. Over a period of time, we develop the capacity to respond to a situation, instead of instinctively reacting.

The Science of Breath

While we cannot consciously regulate processes like heart rate or digestion, we have the extraordinary ability to control our breath, an autonomic function. An expanding body of research and literature emphasises that many health issues, including asthma, anxiety, attention deficit hyperactivity disorder, psoriasis, and more, can be alleviated or even reversed by making conscious adjustments to our inhalation and exhalation patterns. These practices empower us with tools to influence our own nervous and immune systems, manage stress, and address related conditions by fostering emotional control and enhancing athletic performance. They operate on multiple levels, affecting our physiology by stimulating the parasympathetic nervous system and our psychology by sculpting the brain, thereby shaping our moods, thoughts, and behaviors.

Dr Herbert Benson, a Harvard-trained American medical doctor and pioneering figure in mind-body medicine, founded the Mind/Body Medical Institute at Massachusetts General Hospital in Boston. His contributions include several scientific publications and books, notably *The Relaxation Response* (1975), a New York Times bestseller. His simple yet effective technique for triggering the body's inherent 'relaxation response' has helped millions overcome various health challenges, such as mild anxiety, depression, high blood pressure, insomnia, anger issues, and headaches.

In the early 1980s, with the guidance of the Dalai Lama, the spiritual leader of Tibet, Dr Herbert Benson and his team embarked on a journey through the various monasteries in Northern India. What they discovered was astounding: through their unique breathing and meditative practices (tummo), the monks were able to raise the temperatures of their fingers and toes by as much as 17 degrees Fahrenheit. This groundbreaking research was even published in the prestigious scientific journal, *Nature*. In 1985, the meditation team recorded a video of monks using their body heat to dry cold, wet sheets. For most untrained individuals, such frigid conditions would lead to uncontrollable shivering. However, steam began rising from the sheets as the monks harnessed their body heat during meditation, and the sheets dried in about an hour. Further studies documented monks spending a winter night on a rocky ledge 15,000 feet high in the Himalayas, where temperatures dropped to zero degrees Fahrenheit. Wearing only woolen or cotton shawls, the monks quickly fell asleep and didn't huddle together or shiver. They slept soundly until dawn and then walked back to their monastery.

In the early 2000s, a Dutchman known as the 'Iceman', Wim Hof, made headlines by running a half-marathon through the snow in the Arctic Circle, shirtless and barefoot. He also submerged himself in a bath filled with ice for an impressive one hour and 52 minutes without experiencing hyperthermia or frostbite. Over the course of a decade, he shattered 26 world records, each more baffling than the last, effectively challenging established medical norms. In 2011, researchers at Radboud University Medical Center in the Netherlands conducted a study on Wim Hof. They concluded that it was indeed possible to voluntarily influence the autonomic nervous system and immune response through breathing practices, concentration, and meditation. In an unprecedented experiment, they injected an endotoxin, a component of E. coli, into his arm. Exposure to such bacteria typically induces severe symptoms like headaches, fevers, vomiting, and flu-like conditions. However, Wim Hof displayed no signs of fever or nausea and instead, he emerged perfectly healthy. This groundbreaking study, published in the Proceedings of the National Academy of Sciences (PNAS), essentially rewrote biology textbooks, demonstrating that the autonomic nervous system and the innate immune system, once believed to be beyond voluntary control, could indeed be influenced through the practice of specific techniques acquired in short-term training programs.

Throughout history, Yoga gurus have exhibited remarkable control over their bodily functions, pushing the boundaries of what was once thought impossible. Tirumalai Krishnamacharya, often regarded as the father of modern yoga, astounded observers in the 1930s when he demonstrated his ability to stop his own heartbeat. Physicians present during that time were unable to detect his heart beating for over a minute. Swami Rama, another prominent figure, dedicated his life to bridging the gap between science and spirituality. Guided by his master's suggestion, he came to the United States and participated in groundbreaking experiments that reshaped scientific understanding of the connection between the mind and the body. In controlled laboratory conditions, he showcased precise conscious control over autonomic physical responses and mental functions that were previously believed to be beyond human control. Swami Rama could halt his heart's pumping of blood for a remarkable 17 seconds. He could also produce a ten-degree temperature difference between different parts of his palm and voluntarily maintain specific brain wave patterns as needed. He transitioned through various brain wave states: from predominantly active beta waves associated with a conscious state, to the more relaxed alpha waves, and even into theta waves linked to unconscious states. Remarkably, he could recall everything that transpired in the room during these seemingly altered states. His groundbreaking work received extensive coverage in numerous publications, journals, and newspapers across the United States.

On the recommendation of his doctor, science journalist and author, James Nestor, reluctantly decided to attend a breathing class with the hope of improving his deteriorating lung function and finding mental tranquility. It was an introductory course to Sudarshan Kriya, a transformative breathing technique. To his own surprise, he experienced a profound sense of well-being, which eventually led to his authorship of the New York Times Bestseller, *Breath*.

Sudarshan Kriya, the practice he undertook, has been the subject of research at prestigious institutions like Harvard and Yale. A study published in the Harvard Business Review revealed that participants who engaged in SKY breath meditation enjoyed a range of mental health benefits, including improved social connectedness, positive emotions, lower stress levels, reduced depression, and enhanced mindfulness. Additionally, a study involving veterans from Iraq and Afghanistan who grappled with trauma found that SKY breath meditation not only normalised their anxiety levels after just one week but also continued to provide mental health benefits a full year later.

James Nestor's research demonstrates that even minor adjustments to our breathing patterns can have significant impacts, such as boosting athletic performance, revitalising internal organs, mitigating issues like snoring, allergies, asthma, and autoimmune diseases, and even strengthening the spine. These outcomes, once considered implausible, have now been substantiated by modern scientific research.

Nestor further delves into the science behind breathing practices, explaining that the right nostril functions like a gas pedal. When you primarily inhale through this nostril, circulation speeds up, your body temperature rises, and key indicators such as cortisol levels, blood pressure, and heart rate all increase. This occurs because breathing through the right nostril activates the sympathetic nervous system, often associated with the 'fight or flight' response, which heightens the body's alertness and readiness. Additionally, this breathing pattern directs more blood flow to the opposite hemisphere of the brain, particularly the prefrontal cortex, which plays a role in logical decision-making, language processing, and cognitive functions.

Inhaling through the left nostril, on the other hand, serves as a kind of brake system, countering the accelerator-like effect of right-nostril breathing. The left nostril is closely linked to the parasympathetic nervous system, often referred to as the body's 'rest-and-relax' side. This type of breathing leads to a lowering of body temperature, reduced blood pressure, a cooling effect on the body, and a decrease in anxiety levels. Left-nostril breathing also shifts blood flow to the opposite side of the prefrontal cortex, specifically the right hemisphere, which is associated with creative thinking, emotional processing, the formation of mental abstractions, and handling negative emotions.

To maintain optimal efficiency, our bodies require a delicate balance between states of action and relaxation, between daydreaming and rational thought. This balance is influenced by the nasal cycle and may even be controlled by it. Notably, there is a yoga practice dedicated to manipulating the body's functions through controlled breathing via the nostrils. This practice is commonly known as 'nadi shodhana', which translates from Sanskrit to 'channel purification', or more informally, 'alternate nostril breathing'.

In summary, several studies and research supports the notion that altering our breathing patterns can significantly influence how we feel. The responsibility for how we wish to feel and how vibrantly and joyfully we want to live ultimately lies within our control, or rather, in our breath.

* * *

Practical Exercise

- Sit in a comfortable cross-legged position with your eyes closed, spine tall, and chest open.
- Focus your attention on the outer edges of your feet, feeling the sensation of them against the mat. Maintain your concentration on this sensation for a few moments.

- Shift your awareness to your sit bones, grounding into the mat. Explore this sensation and notice if one sit bone feels heavier than the other. Keep your attention steady for a few seconds.
- Bring your attention to your arms, specifically your hands on your knees. Dive deeper by questioning which part of your hand is in contact with your knee—is it the front, the back, the forearm, or the wrist? Hold your focus for a few moments.
- Delicately sense the subtle touch of your eyelids resting gently on your face. Maintain your attention on this sensation for a few seconds.
- Become mindful of your breath, noticing the tactile feeling as it flows in and out of your nostrils during inhalation and exhalation. Keep your attention stable for a few moments.

Upon concluding this practice, you will experience a shift in your mental state from restlessness to a sense of centredness and grounding. These practices will also help us develop and fortify essential mental capacities including:

- The ability to choose our focal point.
- The skill to shift and maintain attention on our chosen point.
- The capacity to channel energy and activate different areas of the body through the power of our attention.

- The potential to rewire the brain. Each of our thoughts and actions leaves a neural imprint, and with repetition, these pathways become stronger and more ingrained.

Om purnamadah purnamidam purnat
purnamudacyate
purnasya purnamadaya purnamevavasisyate.

(Om, That is whole, this is whole. From the whole,
the whole emerges.
Having drawn out the whole from the whole, the
whole alone remains.)
— **Isavasyopanisad**

Chapter 3

YAMAS

Ashtanga Yoga: A Brief Introduction

The mind can be likened to a garden. And just like a gardener regularly clears out the weeds and prunes the garden, we too have to regularly weed out and prune kleshas (afflictions)—avidya (ignorance), asmita (ego), raga (attraction), dvesha (dislike), and abhinivesha (fear) as they are the source of anger, delusion, greed, jealousy, bitterness, and hatred that disrupts the harmony of our mind.

And similar to how a farmer employs fertiliser to enrich the soil, we need to cultivate our inner landscape with bhavanas (nurturing attitudes) given to us by Maharishi Patanjali. These include maitre (friendliness), karuna (compassion), mudita (goodwill), and upekshanam (equanimity). It is through this nurturing that the seeds of concentration can blossom into flowers of meditation, spreading their sweet fragrance across every dimension of our lives.

To achieve the same, Maharishi Patanjali has laid out a systematic path, known as ashtanga or the eight limbs, along with the raison d'etre of practice—cultivating viveka, the sword of discerning wisdom that can cut through the mesh of ignorance that creates suffering.

The Eight Limbs of Ashtanga Yoga

The eight limbs of Ashtanga yoga are as follows:

1. Yamas (moral restraints)
2. Niyamas (ethical observances)
3. Asana (postures)
4. Pranayama (breath regulation)
5. Pratyahara (withdrawal of senses)
6. Dharana (concentration)
7. Dhyana (meditation)
8. Samadhi (absorption)

Meditation as a Holistic Practice

Most people think of meditation as something that needs to be done 20 minutes a day and then carry on with the rest of their lives. However, the effectiveness of those 20 minutes of meditation is significantly influenced by how we think, speak, and act throughout the rest of the day.

If we have spent the entire day in a state of agitation and reactivity and then abruptly shift to meditation, we might force ourselves to sit through the allocated 20-minutes, but our body and mind will still be restless and agitated. Thus, it is crucial to recognise that every thought, intention, word, and action we engage in has a ripple effect which leaves a residual imprint (vasana) in the deeper recesses of the subconscious mind.

If we explore the eight limbs of yoga, as laid out in the Yoga Sutras, we will find that dhyana or meditation is the 7th limb. In fact, dharana, dhyana, and samadhi, concentration, meditation and absorption, collectively termed samyama, are considered as the 'inner limbs' of yoga practice.

Ethical principles, or 'yamas', and observances, or 'niyamas', set us on the path to cultivating a harmonious mental landscape where meditation can naturally emerge. It is important to understand that we cannot actively 'do meditation; instead, we need to create a conducive mental environment that allows the meditative state to naturally manifest.

Yamas and Niyamas: Foundation of Yoga Practice

Though mostly ignored and overshadowed by the flashy and flamboyant third limb, asana, which makes its way on Instagram posts and covers of magazines, yamas and niyamas, the first two limbs of Ashtanga yoga, form the foundational aspects of yoga practice.

These two limbs serve as our moral compass, directing our actions. Without them, the pursuit and practice of other limbs can potentially sharpen negative qualities in an individual. Maharishi Patanjali specified that yamas are considered mahavrtam (great vows), sarvabhauma (universal), and not bound by jati (class), desa (place), kala (time), and samaya (circumstance).

The yamas consist of five key principles: ahimsa (non-violence), satya (truthfulness), asteya (non-stealing), brahmacharya (moderation), and aparigraha (non-possessiveness). Etymologically, 'yam' implies to pull back, making the practice of yamas a discipline of self-control or restraint. These practices offer a path to rise above our survival instinct (abhinivesha klesha) and our need for self-preservation, which are deeply ingrained in our habitual patterns (samskaras) and inherent tendencies (vasanas) that constitute our subconscious nature.

> The yama deals with controlling innate survival tendencies that were useful in animal incarnations but prevent spiritual growth once one attains the human level of existence. Modern men do look like humans, but how many are actually humane?
> —Yogacharya Dr Ananda Balayogi Bhavanani,
> *Understanding the Yoga Darshan*

So, a question that arises here is how do we transcend these obstacles? The answer is through cultivating an attitude of pratipaksha bhavanam. This is a process through which we reverse the tide of negative thoughts by consciously cultivating positive thought patterns. We may not be able to love someone whom we dislike intensely, but we can, intellectually at least, understand that there is always another perspective to the situation. In this way, by releasing judgement and condemnation, we can adopt a softer approach and make allowances for others and their actions.

Yogacharya Dr Ananda Balayogi Bhavanani expresses a similar sentiment in his words, 'The superhuman capacity of a human being is the capacity to make a choice.' Through the practice of yamas, we can exercise this capacity and make a conscious choice to not react to primitive emotions but to respond more consciously and appropriately.

2.33 Vitarka badhane pratipaksha bhavana.

(When disturbed by negative thoughts, cultivate the opposite [positive] ones.)

—Patanjali Yoga Sutras

The Five Yamas

Let's explore the five ethical practices set out in Yamas.

1. **Ahimsa**

   Ahimsa has several interpretations, the most common one being non-violence. Himsa signifies causing harm or even taking another's life, so ahimsa can be seen as refraining from causing pain, non-killing, or avoiding violent tendencies. A famous Sanskrit shloka on ahimsa from the scriptures is as follows:

   Ahimsa paramo dharma, dharma himsa tathaiva cha.
   (Non-violence is the ultimate duty, so too is violence in service of duty)

   The first part of this phrase, ahimsa paramo dharma, was popularised by Mahatma Gandhi.

But in the larger context of Sanatana Dharma, the second line is very important too. It is the moral duty of a person to resort to violence to stop a greater violence or evil. For example, a soldier may have to kill a terrorist to save the lives of many innocent people or a parent may scold their child to prevent them from injuring themselves. All of this is not considered himsa (violence) as the primary intention in these cases is to protect and save. Even in the Bhagavad Gita, Lord Krishna encourages Arjuna, in the middle of the battlefield, to fulfil his dharma duty as a kshtriya warrior class and fight for righteousness, even if it meant killing his beloved grandsire, teachers, uncles, and cousins. Therefore, ahimsa is not just about one's actions but more importantly, about the intention behind the action.

Violence can include the different dimensions of manasika (thoughts) as we can wish ill on others in our minds, vachika (speech) as we can speak unkindly of others, and kayika (physical) as we can hurt others through our actions. In the sutras, Maharishi Patanjali also goes on to include three additional aspects: krita refers to violence done directly by us, karita involves causing violence to be done by us, and anumoditah entails allowing violence to occur in our presence by turning a blind eye. Moreover, allowing someone to be violent towards us also contributes to the perpetuation of violence.

In his book, The Heart of Yoga, T. K. V. Desikachar says, 'Ahimsa is more than just lack of violence. It means kindness, friendliness, and thoughtful consideration of other people and things. We must exercise judgement when thinking about ahimsa. It does not necessarily imply that we should not eat meat or fish or that we should not defend ourselves. It simply means that we must always behave with consideration and attention to others. Ahimsa also means acting in kindness towards ourselves.'

In the book, *Understanding the Yoga Darshan*, Yogacharya Dr Ananda Balayogi Bavanani explores what causes the disturbances and devolutionary thoughts and emotions that lead to ahimsa. The sutras explain that ahimsa is brought about by the sub-human animalistic tendencies towards kama (excessive desire), krodha (rage), lobha (greed), moha (deluded infatuation), mada (pride), and matsarya (jealousy). These aberrant tendencies originate from the depths of our subconscious and unconscious mind. Therefore, the true challenge is not external but within us and only through introspection, we can spiritually evolve.

Another fascinating insight shared by Maharishi Patanjali is that for someone firmly rooted in non-violence, violence dissipates in their presence. Dr Ananda elaborates in his book, remarking, 'Hermitages of the great rishis bore witness to the fact that even natural enemies of the jungle such as tigers and deer lived together in peaceful coexistence within the non-violent aura of the evolved sages. Even violence renounces itself in the face of one who is perfect in non-violent-ness.'

The truth is that on a daily basis, we inflict pain and violence in many unintentional ways. We inadvertently harm small organisms, plants, trees, and even natural elements like oceans and rivers in our daily lives. It is an unavoidable consequence of being human that we will impact the environment around us. However, through awareness of ahimsa, we make a deliberate effort to minimise the harm we cause in our surroundings. But, it's not just external violence we engage in; a significant portion of the pain and violence in our lives originates within ourselves, through our mental chatter and inner narratives. To recognise and address this, we need to cultivate a deep awareness of the patterns of our thoughts, intentions, and emotions as well as our belief systems.

Ahimsa is not mere negative non-injury. It is positive, cosmic love. It is the development of a mental attitude in which hatred is replaced by love. Ahimsa is true sacrifice. Ahimsa is forgiveness. Ahimsa is Sakthi (power). Ahimsa is true strength.

— Swami Sivananda, *Mind: Its Mysteries and Control*

2. **Satya**

    Satya, or truth, holds significant importance for a yoga practitioner. It encompasses being truthful not only in our interactions with the external world but also in our internal self-reflection. The fact is that it requires a lot of courage and brutal honesty to see and accept the reality of things as they are. This requires peeling away the layers of societal and familial conditioning, the stories we tell ourselves, and the excuses we create to justify our shortcomings, be it laziness, greed, emotional instability, procrastination, fear, or limiting self-beliefs. Without such introspection, we risk living unfulfilled lives, constrained by societal expectations and self-deception, which eventually permeate every facet of our existence. Also, in today's age of information and social media, it is equally essential not to propagate rumours or share unverified and erroneous information, as this contributes to the perpetuation of avidya, or ignorance.

    An important point to note is that ahimsa and satya are intertwined principles, with ahimsa preceding satya, emphasising that truth should always be expressed with non-violence at its core. Non-violent communication takes precedence over merely truthful communication. A verse from the Manu Smriti puts it in perspective:

Satyam bruyat priyam bruyat na bruyat satyam
apriyam

Priyam ca nanrutam bruyat esha dharmah
sanatanah.

(Speak the truth, speak in a pleasant manner.
Never speak the truth in an unpleasant manner.
Even if pleasant, do not speak untruth, that is
the path to eternal righteousness.)

The fact is that as we evolve in our practice, the
harmony between ahimsa and satya will naturally
deepen. And though there might be certain
setbacks, we need to set the correct intention
behind our practice and keep the flame of viveka
(discernment) burning bright.

In summary, we must recognise that while
speaking the truth can be exceptionally
challenging and may put us at risk of losing what
we hold most dear, it ultimately liberates us to live
authentic lives. This was exemplified by Mahatma
Gandhi, who championed ahimsa and satya as the
cornerstones of his fight for India's independence
from British rule.

It is also said in the Yoga Sutras that when one
is firmly established in truth, his words become so
potent that whatever he says comes to realisation.
B. K. S. Iyengar elaborates in *Light on the Yoga
Sutras of Patanjali* that most of us think we tell
the truth, but truth is causal, not integrated, and
cellular. For example, when we say, 'I will never eat

chocolates again,' it is essential that every single cell in our body aligns with this intention for it to succeed. Complete and unwavering dedication to our goal, without any cellular disagreement, is what manifests the reality we desire. It is not solely our conscious mind but the unified voice of every cell within us that holds the power to bring our intentions to fruition.

3. **Brahmacharya**

    Brahmacharya, in its literal sense, signifies maintaining continence or sexual restraint. This concept regards sexual energy as a fundamental expression of life force and attributes great power to it. The ancient texts suggest that when we channel this energy properly, we acquire virya, a vital force that bestows knowledge, vigour, and valour. Preserving and harnessing sexual energy leads to the accumulation of virya, which is then transmuted into ojas—a dynamic form of energy akin to personal magnetism. Ojas permeates one's entire personality, strengthens the nervous system, enhances cognitive abilities, and calms the mind. The continued conservation of ojas eventually leads to tejas, an aura or radiant glow that is prominently seen in spiritually evolved people. In the Yoga Sutras, it is said that when a practitioner is firmly established in continence, knowledge, vigour, valour, and energy flow to him.

Sexual energy, being a fundamental expression of the life force, requires us to establish clear boundaries to effectively harness and channel it, just as we do in other aspects of our lives. However, it is important to note that the idea of restricting sexuality is a limited view. Many great sages and yogis of ancient India were married and had families. For instance, the great yogi Vasishta had one hundred children and yet he was called a brahmachari. Even in the recent past, the illustrious names in yoga, from Guruji Krishnamacharya, Guruji T. K. V. Desikachar, Yogamaharishi Dr Swami Gitananda Giri, Guruji B. K. S Iyengar, and Guruji Pattabhi Jois were all householders. This implies that brahmacharya can involve the expression of our sexuality with the appropriate person and at the appropriate time and place, and then it becomes dharma (duty or righteousness).

Moreover, brahmacharya can also be interpreted as living in tune with the brahman, the cosmos or the creative force. In this context, it signifies that we are not merely procreating offspring but are continuously creating words, actions, relationships, and situations. Thus, the practice of brahmacharya calls for us to be conscious of what we are creating in the world and in our lives and allow the creative force to flow through us to realise our highest potential.

4. Aparigraha

Parigraha translates to greed, the tendency to hoard and possess more than necessary. So, aparigraha signifies non-greed, non-grasping, non-hoarding, and the ability to let go, and share love, wealth, and even knowledge with others.

Aparigraha has both physical and emotional aspects to it. It's reflected in the way we maintain our homes and the way we lead our lives. In fact, the manner in which we maintain the surrounding living spaces is often the reflection of the state of our minds. Some people have such cluttered living spaces that there is hardly any place to sit or even stand. One of the reasons for this is that some people struggle to part with items that have long ceased to be useful, such as empty bottles, old clothes, or worn-out belongings. These behaviours symbolise the mind's resistance to letting go of what no longer serves us.

Swami Satchidananda, in his book, *The Yoga Sutras of Patanjali*, notes that aparigraha extends to not accepting gifts, as gifts may come with future obligations. By freeing our minds from these desires and obligations, we gain the capacity for detachment, objectivity, and freedom. Refraining from accepting gifts allows us to maintain neutrality and perceive cause-and-effect relationships more clearly.

Aparigraha also encompasses emotional hoarding, where we cling to past suffering, pain, and unresolved emotions. Even as we mature, we often find ourselves unexpectedly revisiting childhood traumas and grief. Additionally, we tend to tightly grasp our likes (raga), dislikes (dvesha), and ego (ahamkara).

Aparigraha extends to the feeling of ownership and possessiveness we harbour over what we believe is 'ours'—our partners, children, employees, etc. This possessiveness can lead to control issues, entangling our minds in agitation and a sense of entitlement. As we gradually release our hold on people and possessions, we transcend our fears and anxieties, achieving a greater sense of security and wholeness. The Yoga Sutras assure us that the wisdom of the past and future unfolds when we are free from the grip of greed and possessions.

5. Asteya

Asteya, another significant practice, involves the concept of non-stealing. While it may seem quite natural to think, 'Of course, I don't steal' and that this aspect doesn't apply to us, we must expand our understanding of this principle. Asteya extends beyond obvious theft to include even the subtle desire to possess or own something attractive that belongs to another person—be it a house, car, jewellery, or even a partner.

Also, in the digital age, asteya infiltrates our actions at various levels. We often post writings, photographs, and quotes on social media without giving credit to the original source. In the workplace, there are instances where one person does the work, but another receives credit for it. Thus, we can see that theft of ideas, concepts, and information is prevalent everywhere.

In the realm of yoga as well, plagiarism is rampant as we teach, speak and write often without a sense of reverence for tradition or the teachers who imparted knowledge to us. Yoga's growing popularity has led to the misuse of scriptures and teachings without proper credit. Then there's the use of yoga as a marketing tool which further dilutes its true essence. This has given rise to various yoga hybrids, such as beer yoga, ganja yoga, and stoned yoga, which undermine the integrity and sanctity of the term 'yoga'.

So, while it is one thing to objectively see the stealing, we must also look within ourselves to understand the underlying motives for such behaviour. Is it driven by pure greed, exploitation for self-profit and self-aggrandizement, etc.? Or does it stem from the insecurity of competition, due to which we compromise everything including our principles? The sutras assure us that those established in non-stealing effortlessly attract wealth in its truest sense.

Our Power Lies in Our Story

It is essential to realise our inherent capability to empower ourselves through a shift in our perspective on a given situation. In life, our reactions are not solely determined by external events but by the way we interpret and narrate those events. For instance, consider a scenario where five individuals lose their jobs; but each person's response can be drastically different. One might view it as a fresh opportunity to pursue a long-held passion, while another may see it as a chance to further their education. Conversely, someone might spiral into depression, another could turn to alcoholism, and the fifth individual might tragically take their own life. Despite the identical external events, the varying outcomes are shaped by individual perspectives and narratives.

> We must know that it all just comes down to our perspective. The greatest gift that we have is the power to soften and broaden our perspective, to tell ourselves an empowering story.
> — Pratipaksha Bhavanam

However, achieving this transformation necessitates a steadfast commitment to the refinement of our minds. At this juncture, the significance of establishing mimamsa rituals cannot be overstated. Our mental state and the overall quality of our lives are predominantly shaped by our existing patterns. It is imperative to scrutinise these patterns and, if found disempowering, take deliberate steps to forge new ones and diligently adhere to them.

This endeavour calls for a fundamental shift in our competitive mindset. This entails recognising that another person's success does not diminish our own potential for success; in fact, we can all prosper in our respective domains. Every individual we encounter need not be perceived as a threat; rather, they can serve as potential friends, supporters, and allies in our personal growth journey, just as we can be in theirs.

To anchor ourselves in this transformative process, we must remain attuned to our svadharma—our unique life purpose. Armed with a clear sense of our life's mission, we become less susceptible to being perturbed by the accomplishments of others. Instead, we walk our path with unwavering conviction, steadfastly honouring our rendezvous with destiny.

Being Conscious of Our Thoughts

Many of us navigate life without awareness, just completely drowning in the deluge of thoughts and emotions. What we need to recognize is that our minds are ceaseless generators of thoughts, and not every thought is an absolute truth. Each thought is tinged with the imprints of past experiences, swayed by personal preferences and biases, and influenced by our aspirations, expectations, and desires. Also, our thoughts may not even be our own, as we carry the genetic code of our ancestors too. This aspect is perfectly captured by the line, 'We don't see things as they are, we see them as we are.'

To address this, we need to develop the skill to objectively sift through and dissect each thought and check for its validity, and not blindly accept it. Overall, in a life where we are constantly subjected to a barrage of unkind words, misunderstandings, disappointments, frustrations, and health issues, we must find ways to comfort and uplift ourselves and engaging in mindful and compassionate self-dialogue stands as one of the most effective approaches.

* * *

Practical Exercise

- Sit in a comfortable cross-legged position with eyes closed and spine tall and aligned.
- Bring your attention to your breath. Establish a connection with your breath as you observe it for a minute while inhaling and exhaling.
- Slowly begin to count your breaths. Each time you inhale, mentally count one and when you exhale, count one. Similarly count two on the next inhalation and exhalation.
- Continue in this manner, with the mind following every movement of the breath. Try to work up to 45 breaths which might take approximately up to three minutes.
- In the end, release the counting and simply stay with the experience of the breath.

In the beginning, you might find that counting even 15 breaths, which is roughly a minute, presents a huge challenge. But with practice, you will be able to sit for longer periods and build endurance. Each time you realise that your mind has wandered, gently guide it back. Slowly work up to 10 minutes which will be about 150 breaths and later up to 20 minutes, which will be around 300 breaths. At the end of the practice, you would feel calm, centered, and grounded.

Tadejati tannaijati taddure tadvantike
Tadantarasya sarvasya tadu sarvasyasya bahyatah.

(That moves, that moves not. That is afar, that is
even near.
That is inside all this, that is even outside all this.)

—Isavasyopanishad

Chapter 4

NIYAMAS

Niyamas are practices that refine us and facilitate the blossoming of the human spirit through purity, growth, and surrender. Saucha (purity) and santosha (contentment) cleanse and enhance the quality of our inner environment. Through tapas (hard effort) and svadhyaya (self-study), we are encouraged to look within and do the work required to clear out our inner afflictions and by ishvara pranidhana (surrendering to Ishvara) puts on the trajectory to the divine. All of the practices of the yamas and niyamas lead towards antahkarana shuddhi, the cleaning of the inner faculties of mind (manas), intellect (buddhi), and ego (ahamkara), which is necessary for one to be a worthy receptacle of knowledge of self (swarupa jnana).

2.32 Saucha santosha tapah svadhyaya ishvara pranidhanani niyamah.
(Purity, contentment, burning effort, self-study, surrender to the divine are the niyama)

— Patanjali Yoga Sutras

The Five Niyamas

The five niyamas include saucha (purity), santosha (contentment), tapas (burning effort), svadhyaya (self-study), and ishvara pranidhana (surrender to Ishvara). We will explore these in detail in the following sections.

1. **Saucha**

    Saucha refers to our commitment towards upholding purity. Generally, many believe that purity is limited to the rituals of daily bathing or teeth brushing, and while such activities make up the physical aspect (kayika) of purity, there are also the thought (manasika) and the speech (vachika) dimensions to purity. There is also the aspect of external purity, which includes the environment and space that we live and work in, as well as what we consume through our five senses. Thus, it is vital to be conscious of what we let into our mind-body space.

    Let's look at the different ways we consume. The food we consume isn't just sustenance; it is information that affects our hormones, gene expression, and overall metabolism. It profoundly impacts our mental state as well. Therefore, it is important to consider how and where our food is grown, its nutritional and spiritual value, as well as its effects on our body and mind.

    Certain dietary choices, such as excessive sugar, processed foods, white flour, and fried foods, can be detrimental, leading to increased inflammation and stress hormone levels. Consuming a diet high in sugar, for instance, triggers the release of cortisol, the stress hormone. Chronic inflammation, caused by poor dietary choices, can disrupt our immune system, deplete energy, overload detoxification processes, and even alter gene expression, increasing the risk of various diseases.

The way we consume our food is equally important. While eating out or opting for takeaways has become a trend, preparing our meals at home with love, with full knowledge of the ingredients and their freshness and quality remains the best way to ensure their purity. It is important to realise that the raw materials for our body's growth and maintenance, including cells, organs, tissues, skin, and even brain cells, come from the food we consume.

Our dietary considerations don't stop at food alone. The information, entertainment, and external stimuli we allow into our lives also impact our mental landscape. In today's information age, being conscious of what we feed our minds and how much we consume is crucial. The constant influx of information through digital devices can be overwhelming. All of this information, whether wanted or not, leaves an imprint on our minds, affecting our mental health, motivation, and overall well-being.

Moreover, practising purity extends to the skincare products we use. With a little effort, we can ensure that the ingredients and finished products we apply to our bodies are cruelty-free and haven't been tested on animals. Conscious consumerism also extends to checking whether the everyday products we use, from shoes to garments, are ethically produced and not linked to child labour or forced labour. Many responsible companies strictly prohibit such practices and maintain ethical standards in their manufacturing processes.

When it comes to purity, a few other things to consider are as follows:

i. **Examine Your Core Relationships**

    Take a closer look at your fundamental relationships. Are you clear and sincere in understanding the role these relationships play in your personal growth and journey toward realising your full potential? Or do you find yourself holding onto toxic relationships due to societal pressures? It is essential to assess whether your relationships contribute positively to your life or hinder your progress.

ii. **Evaluate the Energy You Allow**

    Pay attention to the people and energies you allow into your inner circle. Do these individuals uplift and inspire you, or do they drain your energy and enthusiasm? Your inner circle has a profound impact on your path towards self-realization and your ability to express your highest potential.

iii. Assess Your Work and Life Alignment

Consider the purity of the time and energy you invest in your work. Is it aligned with your inner calling and your unique path (sva-dharma)? Or are you solely pursuing it because your education qualified you for it, and it provides financial security?

iv. Unconditional Love for Your Children

Reflect on your relationship with your children. Do you love them unconditionally, accepting them for who they are? Or does your love come with expectations based on your unfulfilled dreams? Can you offer unwavering support and love regardless of the career, lifestyle choices, or gender identity they pursue? These questions encourage self-reflection and help you gauge the purity and clarity of various aspects of your life and relationships.

Saucha is not just a tool for classifying people and things as pure or impure, as our minds often tend to do. Instead, it serves as an invitation to embrace the state of sakshi bhava (the witnessing consciousness). In this state, we relinquish identification, judgement, and blame, allowing us to maintain a stance of impartial awareness. This approach enables us to witness and embrace everything that arises in our minds without reacting.

All our yoga practices are oriented toward nurturing this non-judgmental awareness. It is from this open and serene space that we can embrace life as it unfolds, in its purest form, without staining each experience with our biases, preconceptions, expectations, and judgements. It is from this space that wisdom insights, heightened concentration (dharana), and profound meditation (dhyana) naturally arise. Maharishi Patanjali also says that once we get a taste of this state of pure awareness, we are bestowed with gifts such as a joyful mind, enhanced focus, and mastery over the senses, making us fit to receive the highest vision—atma darshana (the vision of the soul). Furthermore, we also need to align ourselves with the chathur bhavana, which encompasses attitudes of friendliness (maitre), goodwill (mudita), compassion (karuna), and equanimity (upekshanam). These attitudes are essential for maintaining a balanced disposition and mental peace. We will delve into each of them more comprehensively in the following sections.

i. Maitre

Maitre embodies the authentic radiance of friendliness that permeates our being and

extends out to everyone and everything
we encounter. This means extending our
friendliness to everyone who crosses our
paths, from the security guards in our
residential areas to the strangers on the
street. Simply put, the practice of yoga
encourages us to be a vishwamitra (friend of
the universe).

The practice urges us to continually
expand our sense of community, starting
from our immediate family and gradually
encompassing friends, colleagues, and
the larger community we are a part of.
Ultimately, it should extend further to
encompass the entire universe and all
its inhabitants, whether living beings or
inanimate elements like plants, rivers, oceans,
and mountains. This even includes people
we may not particularly like or care about.
The real challenge lies in maintaining an 'open
heart'. While it's easy to be friendly with
those we already consider friends and people
we like, it is certainly more challenging when
it comes to extending our love to someone
we believe has hurt or betrayed us. However,
this is where the essence of yoga practice
shines. We must remember that we haven't
experienced life from their perspective,
making it unfair to judge their actions. Our
task is simply to accept them as they are. It
is important to understand that suffering

often stems from resistance or an inability to accept, and by shifting into a space of acceptance, we can release our own suffering more swiftly.

ii. Karuna

Karuna refers to the natural flow of the empathetic energy that awakens within us when we encounter the suffering of fellow humans, animals, or nature. It manifests as a profound compassion for the pain of others.

Whether we read about the hardships of women and children in different cultures, witness individuals enduring torture, see animals mistreated, or forests being cut down to make way for concrete structures, it elicits a genuine connection and emotional response from the heart. Also, this compassion isn't limited to extreme cases; even seeing an elderly person struggling with their groceries can lead to a natural outflow of karuna, which results in our instinctive response to lend a helping hand.

However, we also have to take into account that our minds have the tendency to discriminate on the basis of caste, race, ethnicity, or religion. Therefore, we need to practice to transcend these artificial boundaries and embrace humanity as a whole. Through a transformative process, our compassion may lead us to become animal rights activists, environmental advocates, or champions of various causes, each expressing the energy of karuna in their own unique way.

iii. Mudita

Mudita is the experience of empathetic joy that emanates from us as the energy of goodwill and cheerfulness when we witness the joy of others. Typically, when friends and colleagues achieve something significant, such as a coveted raise, a great career opportunity, or an award, our immediate response may be tinged with envy or insecurity. The first step is to acknowledge this initial reaction truthfully, saying to ourselves, 'Yes, I feel envious,' while keeping our response in check. This reaction is rooted in our survival instinct, known as abhinivesha klesha. However, we can educate our minds not to feel threatened or insecure just because someone excels in a particular area or receives a great opportunity. The world is abundant enough to accommodate and provide for everyone. With this understanding, our hearts can genuinely swell with goodwill when we witness the achievements and good fortune of others. It also serves as an inspiration for our own individual pursuits. In my yoga classes, I often encounter students with varying body structures, making some asanas easier for some than others. Instead of feeling inadequate when observing others' accomplishments, I encourage them to draw inspiration from these achievements and channel that energy to enhance their strengths and focus on their progress.

iv. Upekshanam

One of the most beautiful qualities to cultivate is upekshanam and it refers to the capacity of our hearts to accommodate and embrace vastly contrasting life experiences, like success and failure, fame and shame, excitement and boredom, wealth and penury, all without being completely overwhelmed by them.

In the Bhagavad Gita, specifically in verse 2.48, Lord Krishna imparts one of the most renowned definitions of yoga, saying, 'samatvam yoga uchyate.' The term 'samatvam' closely aligns with the concept of upekshanam, and yoga is thus described as the ability to maintain equilibrium and rootedness when confronted with life's dualities or dvandvas. We frequently measure our worth in terms of success or failure, profit or loss, victory or defeat. This continuous evaluation often leads to a rollercoaster of emotional turbulence, causing us to lose touch with our inner stability. In the pursuit of upekshanam, we liberate ourselves from the relentless sway of these dualities and rediscover the serenity within.

How Do We Cultivate Upekshanam?

To attain upekshanam, the quality of equanimity, we require the objectivity that witnessing our experiences provides. This objectivity enables us to view life through the lens of the intellect and comprehend the broader picture of existence. Life's difficult moments, such as upheavals or crises, can be understandably overwhelming, and feeling sadness, disappointment, or bitterness is a normal reaction.

Thus, before we jump to conclusions like 'This always happens to me' or 'I have no luck', we should practise pratipaksha bhavanam, which involves adopting an expanded or even opposing perspective. We can do this through a conscious effort to see life from a broader perspective and acknowledge its various dimensions and then realise the countless blessings we have received. It could be having caring children, a supportive spouse, wonderful parents, a fulfilling childhood, innate intelligence that eased our educational journey, steadfast friends, or excellent physical health. These are all significant blessings, but we must first see and then acknowledge them as the precious gifts they are. Otherwise, it is easy for the mind to take these blessings for granted and focus solely on the one dimension of life that isn't going as planned and then sink into negativity. It is similar to fixating on a tiny black dot on a white shirt while ignoring the expanse of white around it. Simply put, an unconscious and untrained mind tends to magnify the negative aspects while ignoring the positive ones.

Moreover, it is crucial to cultivate shraddha, or faith, in the grand plan of the universe and not to quickly label events as either good or bad. We must develop a deep inner knowing, gained through witnessing the unfolding course of our lives, that the universe supports us and has a purpose for our journey.

2. Santosha

Santosha, contentment, is the ability to reframe our perspective on life from one of lack to abundance. It encourages us to appreciate and focus on what we have and can achieve, rather than fixating on our deficiencies or limitations. This attitude holds even more significant value in today's world where we are constantly competing and comparing. Santosha encourages us to break free from the self-defeating cycle of measuring our innate self-worth against the strengths of others, which naturally leaves us feeling inadequate and lacking.

A quote that beautifully illustrates this concept:

Everybody is a genius. But if you judge a fish by its ability to climb a tree, it will live its whole life believing it is stupid.

— Albert Einstein

It is crucial to understand that comparison is a significant source of unhappiness in life. As a wise spiritual teacher once said, 'Everyone is happy with their house, car, body or partner, till they see their neighbour's car, house, body or partner!'

This aspect becomes all the more relevant in the current world dominated by social media. And being a great platform for self-expression, it can also expose us to images of individuals striking beautiful yoga poses, winning awards, or flaunting seemingly flawless bodies. This exposure often leads to feelings of inadequacy and self-doubt. We become engrossed in the pursuit of keeping up with others, losing sight of our own values, strengths, and life's purpose. Consequently, we find ourselves trapped in a whirlpool of dissatisfaction, frustration, low energy, depression, and reduced productivity.

Hence, it is essential to focus on our strengths and find satisfaction from the entire journey, embracing its struggles and setbacks. When I reached the summit of Mt. Kinabalu in East Malaysia in February 2019, the actual moment at the top felt somewhat anticlimactic. We only had a few minutes to snap hurried pictures. The true joy and satisfaction sprang from the entire journey and overcoming the challenges of this journey. It stemmed from weeks and months of rigorous training, meticulous research on suitable clothing and weather conditions, shopping, and packing. The real fulfilment came from delving deep within and finding the resilience to keep on going, step after step, through the darkness with only headlamps to guide us, all in a completely unfamiliar and mountainous terrain.

Likewise, in life, we wait till we acquire the perfect car or the perfect house before we give ourselves permission to feel happy. Santosha teaches us to find satisfaction and contentment in where we are now and cherish every step we take toward our ultimate goals. And instead of constantly comparing our lives to others' or pursuing an elusive idea of perfection, our focus should shift to honouring our svadharma, our unique path, purpose, and responsibilities that bring meaning and direction to our life. We need to stop fixating on what's lacking in our lives and embrace the present moment. It is essential to recognise the progress we have made, despite the obstacles we have encountered along the way. And a key aspect of contentment is the ability to 'see' what we have by consciously cultivating a gratitude practice. Once our hearts become full of gratitude, contentment is a natural outflow.

A close friend and yoga teacher, who had just come back from a doctor's visit where he received the unsettling news of a muscle tear, shared a remarkable perspective with me. He said, 'I am just so grateful that there is no major sacroiliac joint damage.' Only through years of practicing santosha allows us to react in this manner and makes us understand that things could always be worse, that everything and everyone can disappear in an instant, and that nothing is guaranteed. Every aspect we tend to take for granted, from our ability to move, speak, eat, and digest, to our cognitive abilities and having a body free from pain, even the simple act of breathing, can be abruptly taken away. As long as the mind is always in the grip of desires and discontent, it cannot allow contentment to flourish. This is why cultivating santosha is significant and as Maharishi Patanjali assures us, supreme happiness awaits us on this path.

3. Tapas

Tapas, derived from the word 'taap', which signifies heat, refers to the heat of effort. It is the unwavering commitment and intense self-discipline of tapas that is essential to do the right thing and not give in to the mind's attractions (ragas) and aversions (dveshas). This discipline empowers us to stand up against our samskaras, which are deeply ingrained patterns of sloth, procrastination, laziness, inertia, indiscipline, indulgence, and the tendency to blame others. These patterns often solidify over the years, and sometimes even lifetimes, becoming formidable barriers to achieving our goals.

The practice of tapas serves as a transformative fire that burns all that is not an authentic part of ourselves, which, in turn, enables our inner light to shine brilliantly. This is similar to how a sculptor chips away at a block of stone to reveal the inherent perfection within the rock. It echoes the sentiment expressed by the renowned Italian sculptor Michelangelo, who once said, 'I saw the angel in the marble and carved until I set him free.'

When we take an objective look at our lives, we will realise that we are constantly operating under the influence of deeply ingrained habitual patterns. These patterns exert a powerful and unyielding grip on our actions. We might repeatedly tell ourselves that we are giving up sugar, but when someone offers us a sweet, it becomes exceedingly challenging to decline. Similarly, we make resolutions to wake up at 5 a.m. every morning for a 20-minute meditation session, yet when the alarm rings, we simply switch it off and go back to sleep. We set targets to visit the gym thrice a week, only to find ourselves creating an array of excuses as to why we cannot go. Sage Vyasa, in his commentary on the Yoga Sutras, says that the yoga of an a-tapasvin (non-tapas person) will not succeed.

In our pursuit of tapas, we are essentially training ourselves to confront discomfort. For instance, during a 10-minute sitting practice, it is common to experience an urge to fidget or scratch within the first minute. This impulse often arises from unconscious patterns of restlessness. Tapas, in this context, involves the capacity to endure this sensation without immediately giving in and moving.

So, why is tapas important? There are often aspects of our lives where we encounter obstacles and feel stagnant. These may manifest as prolonged struggles to reach our desired weight, achieve fitness goals, master a challenging yoga pose like a handstand, or maintain a regular writing routine, such as composing one chapter of a book every week. Such persistent struggles can lead to feelings of restlessness, discontent, and even depression.

To realise the aspirations we have set for ourselves in any area of life, whether it pertains to our diet, fitness, yoga practice, or professional work, tapas becomes essential. It serves as the driving force that empowers us to confront and overcome long-established patterns that may have hindered our progress. The transformation we experience will be directly proportional to the level of tapas we invest in this endeavor. In the Yoga Sutras, Maharishi Patanjali assures us that tapas burns aways impurities of the body, mind, and senses and thus sets us on the path to divinity.

Tapas also encompasses the practice of austerities to attain higher objectives. A notable example is Mahatma Gandhi, whose transformative influence on global political protest is well-recognised. He practised severe austerities, which included fasting, as an integral part of his philosophy of ahimsa (non-violence) and satya (truth) as well as to eliminate his perceived weaknesses. In the process, he awakened his unwavering will and implacable attitude that served to gain India's freedom from the British.

Practice of Tapas

To achieve our goals, practising self-discipline is essential. Consistent routines in various aspects of our lives can pave the way for greater accomplishments.

i. **Tapas of Fasting**

   Fasting one day a week is a great way to restrain our need to indulge in food all the time and curb excessive eating. Whether you want to commit to a dawn-to-dusk fast, a 24-hour fast, intermittent fasting, a water-only fast, or a fruit fast, the key is being committed to your practice.

ii. **Tapas of Diet**

   The commitment towards healthy eating, i.e., a diet devoid of sugar or refined carbohydrates, with reduced meat consumption and an emphasis on vegetables, etc., requires the will of tapas in order to keep it going day after day. The same holds true whether you choose to go vegetarian, vegan, paleo, or keto.

iii. Tapas of Exercise

This involves committing to invest in ourselves and our health by engaging in daily physical activity, be it a 20-minute yoga session every day or five days a week, hitting the gym, hiking, walking 10,000 steps daily, or any other preferred exercise routine.

iv. Tapas of Learning

This refers to pursuing continuous growth and learning, whether it's in yoga, personal development, or our professional life. For this, we need to allocate time each day to read, listen to podcasts, or contemplate, and incorporate this time into our daily schedule, perhaps in the morning or during commutes.

v. Tapas towards Loved Ones

In our busy lives, it is crucial to make time for family, especially elderly parents, uncles, aunts, and close friends who value our connection. And thereby, in an era where it is so easy to neglect our loved ones due to our busy schedules, tapas is needed in order to give undivided attention to people we care about.

Tapas can be applied to any area of our lives where we seek transformation and progress. The essence of tapas lies in how it manifests in our ability to uphold our commitments. Think of it like a dedicated boxer who trains rigorously year-round. All that training must ultimately show in the boxing ring when he faces his opponent. In a similar vein, the tapas we practice should demonstrate its effectiveness when we face challenges. Can we still make it to the gym on a tiring day? Can we resist indulging in sweets when tempted? Can we rise promptly when our morning alarm sounds? It is in these moments that the true test of our tapas unfolds.

Meditation and Tapas

To establish a consistent sitting meditation practice, we must employ tapas to maintain our commitment. This dedication helps us navigate the various obstacles that can hinder our practice, such as procrastination, boredom, sleepiness, and restlessness. When we attempt to focus during meditation, we often contend with a mental assault of restlessness, manifested as the urge to move, itch, or fidget without even consciously recognising it. At times, we may struggle to sit for the prescribed 20 minutes, battling feelings of boredom and inertia. It takes tapas to deliberately direct our thoughts and ignite our curiosity about the profound nature of this practice.

However, before we can make progress, we must identify our adversaries and understand the barriers that stand in our way. This calls for introspection and asking tough questions: What hinders my wisdom and clear perception? What saps my energy? Why do I feel this load on my mind, or why do I feel restlessness? This form of self-inquiry leads us to svadhyaya, the practice of self-study.

4. **Svadhyaya**

Svadhyaya, in a traditional sense, refers to the contemplation of scriptures, but it can also be expanded to mean study (adhyayanam) of ourselves (sva). And this process involves continuous self-reflection, which is one of our greatest capacities as a human being. Self-reflection allows us to engage in introspection, self-analysis, critical examination, and investigation and enables us to see who we are.

While tapas signifies the doing or action-oriented energy, svadhyaya lends a 'knowing' quality. Svadhyaya empowers us to gain insight into our motivations, intentions, weaknesses, and strengths, beginning with an understanding of our own mind. Consider:

- Where does your mind tend to wander? To whom or what does it gravitate?
- What is the default setting of the mind?
- What triggers the mind and what soothes it? What brings it satisfaction and what bores it?

- What does your mind cling to? What does it crave? What is it passionate about?

- What is the predominant tone of your mental chatter? Is it repetitive, judgmental, comparative, or inclined towards complaints and self-pity?

- What emotions are you experiencing at this moment? Is it anger, sadness, frustration, or hopelessness?

- Do you acknowledge your role in situations, or is it always someone else's fault? Do you perceive yourself as a perpetual victim in your own story? Is there a more skilful way to respond, empowering yourself within the situation?

Svadhyaya, in this expanded sense, encourages deep self-awareness and a better understanding of our inner landscape. And as we gain clarity about the workings of our mind, we have the opportunity to establish new, constructive patterns and value systems that support our personal growth. I often encounter individuals who express a strong desire to lose weight, yet their actions contradict their words, as evidenced by the presence of snack packets like biscuits and chocolates by their bedside. It is crucial to recognise that as long as we hold onto a self-image shaped by our imagination, we remain trapped in our current state. To move forward, we must have the ability to identify and address the dysfunctional aspects of our mind with precision. Svadhyaya, marked by its clarity, and supported by the determination of tapas, equips us to transcend years of conditioning and make choices that lead to personal transformation.

As we develop the ability to observe our own minds, we create some distance between ourselves and the events and thoughts occurring within our mental landscape. This process allows us to become less ensnared by our thoughts and emotions. Consequently, we can adopt a more objective standpoint, gain a fresh perspective on our experiences, and intentionally steer our minds towards more positive and constructive states.

Practical Application of Svadhyaya

For instance, if we notice that our mind is often preoccupied with worries about impending deadlines before bedtime, we can employ various techniques, such as jotting down entries in a gratitude journal, engaging in mantra chanting, or practicing a short meditation session with a focus on the breath. These practices help in shifting our mental state to a more tranquil and settled space. Likewise, if we become aware that we wake up feeling uninspired and low-spirited, we can proactively introduce new morning routines involving breathing practices, stretches, and other exercises. These activities trigger the release of feel-good hormones in our body, elevating our mood and overall sense of well-being.

To summarise, Svadhyaya provides us with

a profound understanding of our actions and our emotions along with the underlying causes of our emotions. This practice further enables us to observe how emotions manifest physically, leading to bodily sensations like tension, shallow breathing, or narrowed eyes. Armed with the knowledge of these afflictions, we gain valuable tools to identify the source of our negative emotions and effectively address them.

In the Yoga Sutras, the direction of svadhyaya also encompasses the study of the scriptures that leads to the knowledge of the self. It says svadhyaya leads towards the realisation of God or communion with one's beloved deity (ishtadevata).

5. Ishvara Pranidhana

Ishvara pranidhana is the highest principle that holds us in a space of acceptance. Life can often become difficult and challenging and put us through situations and circumstances where nothing makes sense. In this context, 'Ish' symbolises the mysterious intelligence of the universe, the vital force behind all existence. 'Vara' signifies grace or blessings. Together, 'Ishvara' implies that every moment of our life is a divine blessing from this universal force which is within us all. 'Pranidhana' refers to the act of surrender, wherein we relinquish control over the circumstances of our lives to something greater.

Our suffering often arises from our inability to accept the situations life throws at us. For instance, one of my students endured the heart-wrenching experience of losing her 7-year-old daughter to a rare form of cancer. Another person suffered a miscarriage, losing a long-anticipated baby at five months of pregnancy. Yet another individual, who had a promising life with young children, is battling cancer. Similarly, a close friend is grappling with the tragic loss of both parents in a sudden car accident. I too, personally, underwent the profound pain of losing someone I deeply cherished—the person I have dedicated this book to. Krishna Kumarji was my mentor, spiritual guide, and an essential pillar of my support system, and his passing away occurred most unexpectedly

Life throws numerous challenges our way, including job losses, the end of relationships, the breakdown of our support systems, and situations demanding excruciating decisions. These circumstances often lead us to critical crossroads, where we must make choices that can be emotionally devastating. These decisions may include the heart-wrenching choice to discontinue life support for a loved one or to terminate a much-anticipated pregnancy for medical or other reasons. At times, there are no apparent, logical, or rational solutions to these dilemmas. Such experiences can leave us feeling angry, questioning, bitter, resentful, and filled with self-loathing, accompanied by consuming guilt.

In these moments, the principle of Ishvara pranidhana serves as our sanctuary. Through 'shraddha', or faith, we must discover the capacity within our hearts to surrender the circumstances of our lives to the divine will of Ishvara. This entails embracing humility and acknowledging our limited comprehension of the complexities of karma and the universe. And even though life may appear unfair within the scope of our limited understanding, there exists a profound wisdom in the universe to which we must surrender and maintain faith in a benevolent universe. Over time, this surrender allows us to progress with greater resilience.

Living from a profound connection with Ishvara, we witness how people, events, and circumstances spontaneously align themselves to facilitate our highest growth, almost as if by magic. The practice of tapas, svadhyaya, and ishvara pranidhana sets us on a path toward a state of divinity itself.

I will conclude this section with a quote that beautifully encapsulates this essence.

Every moment life comes at us and we respond. It is in that response that we apply the wisdom of yoga. The question is whether we respond according to raga (like) and dvesha (dislike) or in accordance with our svadharma, what is the right action for us at this moment?

— Manoj Kaimal, *Manasa Yoga*

* * *

Practical Exercises

❖ Saucha, Santosha, Tapas, Svadhyaya, and Ishwara Pranidhana

1. **Svadhyaya (Self-study):**

   Dedicate 20 minutes each day to journaling. Svadhyaya, as a journaling practice, provides a safe space for connecting with our innermost feelings, free from the masks we often wear in our external lives. Throughout our day, we often play specific roles, but through journaling, we can be authentic and honest with ourselves. This process not only helps us establish a connection with the purity (saucha) of our thoughts and actions but also aligns them with our inner purpose (svadharma). Take a moment to ponder: What is my true calling or svadharma? Do my relationships, career, way of life, and attitude align with my svadharma?

   You can choose to journal either in the morning or at night. Journaling in the morning sets a positive and inspired tone for your day, while journaling in the evening allows you to conclude your day with a sense of resolution and serenity, regardless of the day's events.

2. **Tapas (Self-discipline)**

    Reflect on your day and reactions, using this opportunity to sow the seeds of personal growth. For example, if you found yourself snapping at your child in the morning due to time constraints, resolve to better manage your time and reduce morning stress. By consciously formulating and rehearsing new responses in your mind, you initiate the development of new neural pathways in your brain. Gradually, you begin to break free from established disempowering patterns and respond differently. Through the practice of tapas, you can reprogram subconscious patterns from your childhood.

3. **Ishwara Pranidhana (Surrender to a Higher Power)**

    Incorporate positive affirmations into your journaling. Phrases like 'The universe supports my efforts', 'I am exactly where I need to be', and 'Every day I am unfolding into my highest possibilities' act as reminders that soothe and comfort us on a profound level. They also grant us permission to release the burden of feeling solely responsible for every aspect of our lives, reminding us of the supportive hand of the universe guiding our efforts.

❖ **Santosha (Contentment that Stems from Gratitude)**

Make 5-10 journal entries daily expressing gratitude for the past 24 hours. These entries need not capture extraordinary moments but rather the everyday victories that warm your heart. This practice triggers the release of dopamine, a neurotransmitter that keeps you motivated and inspired. It also helps in developing neural pathways that train your brain to recognise the everyday beauty often overlooked, leading to a higher experience of contentment. Cultivating a conscious gratitude mindset leads to deep contentment and counteracts emotions of envy, jealousy, comparison, regret, and victimhood.

❖ **Creating a Blueprint for Life:**

Through saucha and svadhyaya, you can craft a blueprint for your life that aligns with your svadharma. Through santosha, tapas, and ishwara pranidhana, you can manifest this future vision of yourself.

- **Relationships:** With yourself, key individuals (spouse, parents, children, friends, colleagues), society, country, environment, and the universe.
- **Mental Health:** Establish rituals and practices, such as meditation, nature walks,

yoga asanas, chanting, and music, to support your mental well-being.

- **Diet and Fitness:** Set specific goals for diet and fitness, including the number of hours of exercise per week and adherence to dietary plans.

- **Financial and Work Goals:** Define your financial and work objectives.

- **Experiences:** List experiences you seek in life, such as fun, laughter, meaningful connections, deep conversations, moments of intimacy, travel, music, dance, learning, and sharing.

Saktimadhye manah krtva saktim
manasamadhyagam
manasa mana alokya dharayet paramam padam.

(Immerse the mind into the middle of energy and
receive energy into the middle of mind.
Using the mind to contemplate on the experience
of energy, realise that you are, and always were,
one with the universal consciousness.)

—Hathayogapradipika

Chapter 5

ASANA

These days, the words asana and exercise are often used interchangeably, but it's crucial to distinguish between the two. While asana may begin with what appears to be a physical stretch, its essence goes beyond that. One of the definitions of asana is 'asyate iti asana', which means 'that which can be seated upon'. Manoj Kaimal interprets these words to mean that these postures and forms (asanas) serve as a geometrical template (mandalas) for the universal energy, shakti, to take a seat and express itself and for us to experience its presence.

So, while on a surface level, asana practice can indeed involve stretching and strengthening the body, what elevates it to a sacred practice is the profound opportunity it offers to transcend the vagaries of the mind and perceive, connect with, and engage in a dance with the underlying energy reality that constitutes our existence.

Mind-Body-Breath Nexus

The human mind tends to perceive everything as separate entities. However, when we look at the bigger picture, we realise that we are an integral part of a larger continuum that encompasses the entire universe. Similarly, the body is intricately linked to the mind, forming a seamless connection with breath and energy. This perspective is not solely the wisdom of yogis through the ages but also finds support in modern scientific understanding.

In contemporary times, stress is recognised as a significant contributing factor to many diseases. Although stress is primarily experienced in the mind, it eventually takes a toll on the body, resulting in the manifestation of various illnesses. This insight has been echoed down the ages by the yogis.

> The primary cause of diseases which afflict the body is bad thoughts. Whatever you hold in your mind will be produced in the physical body. Any ill-feeling or bitterness towards another person will at once affect the body and produce some kind of disease in the body. Intense passion, hatred, longstanding bitter jealousy, corroding anxiety, fits of hot temper actually destroy the cells of the body and induce disease of the heart, liver, kidneys, spleen and stomach. Violent fits of hot temper do serious damage to the brain cells, throw poisonous chemical products into blood, produce general shock and depression and suppress the secretion of gastric juice, bile and other digestive

juices in the alimentary canal, drain away your energy, vitality, induce premature old age and shorten life.
— Swami Sivananda, *Mind: Its Mysteries and Control*

Everything that we feel and experience in the moment flows through our bloodstream, settles in our bodies as muscular patterns, as well as in the myofascial tissue. It also influences the environment around a cell that signals genes and thus the genetic structure of the human body. At Manasa Yoga, the body is seen as the subconscious mind where deep emotions are housed. When our boss shouts at us and we cannot respond back to defend ourselves, our partner accuses us without giving us a chance to explain, a friend cuts us off because of a misunderstanding, all these unexpressed emotions render us feeling helpless and hopeless and remains frozen in the body.

This wisdom of the inherent non-divisiveness of body and mind forms the psychological, physiological and spiritual underpinning of yoga.
— Manoj Kaimal, *Manasa Yoga*

So, we can see that not only physical issues but also the negative emotions we carry, such as frustration, guilt, betrayal, sadness, or feelings of unworthiness that may have accumulated during our childhood due to unconscious parenting or childhood abuse, become ingrained in our muscles at a cellular level. Additionally, the trauma we experience as adults, whether it's from job loss, the end of a relationship, or a pervasive sense of dissatisfaction and meaninglessness in our daily lives, also leaves a mark on our energy body. This often manifests as a sense of heaviness, dullness, low energy, lethargy, and a lack of enthusiasm. It robs us of the capacity to experience joy and laughter.

It is in this context that our asana practice plays a vital role. Asana practice assists in releasing the stored trauma and blocked energy in our bodies. It becomes a crucial component of holistic health because it encompasses working with the body, breath, energy, and the subconscious mind, addressing the deep-rooted aspects of trauma, guilt and shame for our well-being.

What Is Asana?

When we refer to Maharishi Patanjali's Yoga Sutras, the first and possibly the most widely quoted sutra on asana is:

> 2.46 Sthira sukham asanam.
>
> (Asana is a steady comfortable posture.)

In contrast to the above definition of asana, the first thing that comes to people's mind at the mention of the word asana is a body twisted like a pretzel as seen on Instagram or Facebook. However, any attempt to forcibly twist or contort our bodies into positions in pursuit of preconceived notions of what poses should look like— such as aiming to touch one's head to the knee in seated forward bends, toes in standing forward bends, or head to feet in backbends—deviates from the original intention of yoga practice. This approach tends to be ego-driven, primarily aimed at soothing the ego by striving to reach endpoints that are often unattainable. In such a practice, the mind tends to be preoccupied with the physical discomfort or pain experienced during these contortions, or it becomes fixated on the passing of time, impatiently awaiting the end of the pose. Such an approach doesn't foster the qualities of 'sthira' (steadiness) and 'sukham' (ease) in the practice. By the end of the session, our minds are often left in a restless and agitated state, potentially even worse off than when we initially started.

What we need to realise is the purpose of asana practice is to expand our perspective beyond a narrow focus on the physical shape of the body. While the physical form is where we typically begin, it is important not to remain fixated solely on it. Our asana practice can be a space for deep connection and rejuvenation as we engage in a samvada conversation, an exchange of information, through deep listening, receiving insights and appropriately responding with love.

An Introduction to Gunas

The universe, known as 'prakriti' in yoga philosophy, comprises both the manifest and unmanifest aspects and is structured around three fundamental forces, known as 'trigunas'. These three forces are:

1. **Sattva:** It represents equilibrium and serenity and is linked to the light of awareness. When sattva is predominant in the mind, it tends to manifest qualities such as virtue, knowledge, non-attachment, non-judgmental thinking, lack of possessiveness,

empathy, and supportiveness. Sattva increases when we seek knowledge, strive to enhance awareness, maintain an open-minded approach, and engage in learning.

2. **Rajas:** It symbolises dynamism, action, passion, and movement.

3. **Tamas:** It represents inertia, stagnation, and the power of contraction in prakriti. When tamas dominates the mind, it can lead to qualities such as the absence of virtue, a lack of empathy, reduced supportiveness, clinging to preconceived notions and prejudices, a desire to enforce authority, and a need for control.

The interplay and balance of these three gunas define the essential qualities of individuals or things in the universe. Importantly, as humans, we possess the unique ability to influence and shift the delicate equilibrium of these gunas in our bodies and minds through our lifestyle choices and thought patterns.

The ultimate aim of yoga, leading to the elevated state known as 'kaivalya', is to transcend these gunas and become 'gunatita', which means rising above the influence of the gunas to attain a state of pure awareness and liberation.

Asana and Gunas

According to Manoj Kaimal, asana practice can be viewed through the lens of the gunas. As mentioned, asana, at its core, is about cultivating stability or 'sthira'. This implies that when something requires stabilisation, there must be an element of instability within it. This element of instability is often associated with rajas, which represents energy. Left unchecked, rajas can lead to mindless spinning and even create a sense of inner vertigo until it exhausts itself. It is important to note that the energy of rajas is neutral, and it can be influenced by either sattva or tamas.

In our asana practice, all three gunas—sattva, rajas, and tamas—will always be present, and we can consciously observe their interplay and influence them. The desired direction is for sattva, representing the light of awareness, to guide rajas. In cases where tamas dominates rajas, we tend to fixate on specific end points, like striving to touch our head to our knee or palm to the floor, without much awareness or understanding of whether our bodies are prepared for such postures. This approach carries the risk of injury.

On the other hand, a sattva dominant approach in our practice always encourages us to explore and connect with the holistic experience of the asana. It prioritises understanding the state of the body, breath, mind, and energy rather than blindly pursuing end points. When we infuse the principles of yamas and niyamas into our asanas, our practice naturally evolves into a sattvic practice. Without these ethical and moral guidelines, the practice can lean toward an ego-driven tamasic approach, leading to feelings of discontent, envy, jealousy, and even violent thoughts directed at ourselves.

The essence of sattva is reflected in a pleasant, light, and sweet state of mind, characterised by equanimity despite the external drama. In this state, we experience sukham, a sense of ease, harmony, and pleasant consciousness. Therefore, in the context of asana, it is not merely about the physical shape; what truly matters is the inner state. To be considered an authentic asana, a shift toward a sattva-dominant state needs to take place.

Asana and Dhyana

The concept of meditation often conjures up an image of someone sitting cross-legged with closed eyes. In contrast, we typically associate asana with posture and dynamism. This separation is a byproduct of our conditioned perspective, wherein meditation is linked with sitting and stillness, while asana is connected with posture and activity.

Yet, when we delve into the essence of asana, which represents just one limb of Ashtanga yoga, we discover that it embodies the other limbs as well. An action becomes an asana only when practised in harmony with the yamas and niyamas. For example, adherence to the yamas, such as ahimsa (non-violence) and satya (truth), is integral to the practice. If we merely push our bodies to conform to a predetermined shape without respecting our current state of practice, health, or body, we forsake non-violence and truth, leading to potential injuries and dissatisfaction. Similarly, the niyamas of tapas, saucha, santosha, svadhyaya, and ishwara pranidhana must be reflected in our asana practice. To deepen our asana practice necessitates significant tapas—an unwavering commitment to continuous practice over an extended period, characterised by persistence and respect.

Asana practice also serves as an ongoing process of svadhyaya, a form of self-study. By deeply observing, attentively listening, and objectively witnessing the body, breath, and mind, we begin to perceive them as they are. Most of the time, we are immersed in our self-created narratives and identify strongly with the body and mind, labelling ourselves as stiff, overweight, weak, or burdened with issues like anxiety or anger management.

Using the analogy of waves in the ocean, we come to understand that the emotional turmoil we experience resembles the rising waves of a stormy sea. As these waves settle, we gain glimpses of the beauty, stillness, and expansiveness at the ocean's depths. Similarly, as the turbulence in our minds subsides through our asana practice, we have the opportunity to taste the inherent peace, joy, and stillness within us. This revelation aligns with the teachings of Maharishi Patanjali in the Yoga Sutras. As the waves of disturbances in the chitta (consciousness) settle, the svarupa of the true self—the drashtu (seer)—gets avasthanam (established).

One remarkable aspect of yoga practice is its experiential nature. Terms like 'inner peace' and 'inner joy' are abundant on social media, but they remain mere words until we embark on our yoga journey. Through consistent practice, these experiences come to life, gaining deeper significance. Even if they are fleeting, these experiences offer glimpses of our universal nature—expansive, peaceful, and accommodating. These moments leave imprints, known as vasanas, in our subconscious mind. Over time, with continuous practice, these impressions become deeply ingrained as samskaras, influencing our personality traits. Consequently, during times of emotional turbulence or meltdowns, we don't identify as strongly with them. Our samskaras and vasanas, honed through years of practice, come to our aid, reminding us that our true nature is peaceful, non-judgmental, and grounded, while the current emotional turmoil is only a temporary aberration.

As our awareness expands, we realise that we are not confined to the limitations of the body and mind. We possess the capacity to observe, work with, and transform them consciously through our own will.

Scope of Asana: From Form to Formless

2.47 Prayatna saithilya ananta samapattibhyam.
(Perfection in asana is achieved through the relaxation of focus on the effort and the immersion of awareness in the infinite.)
— Patanjali Yoga Sutras

To hold our body in postures, it requires a conscious effort to overcome the ingrained tendencies of tamas, which often manifest as tight hamstrings, hips, a stiff spine, rounded shoulders, and a closed chest. However, once we have established the posture, Maharishi Patanjali encourages us to release the physical effort and turn our focus inwards. We shift our focus from the physical form of the posture to experience the formless energy reality of our being, characterised by feelings of spaciousness, vibration, and light.

The process of applying the intense effort (prayatnam) in an asana starts with a focus on physical alignment: the placement of hands and feet, maintaining square hips, activating fingers, engaging the abdomen, and steadying the gaze. Intense effort in an asana is required to go against conditioned patterns of the untrained body built over years of inactivity. However, once this alignment is achieved, practitioners are encouraged to observe the restlessness of the mind, which constantly seeks to attain a specific outcome. This restlessness often manifests in fidgety body movements in the name of making adjustments. These movements are driven by the interplay of the gunas, with tamas (inertia) dominating rajasic (active) tendencies as they strive to achieve a predetermined idea.

What is unfortunate is that many students remain confined to the physical aspects of asana practice, limiting its profound potential to something superficial. This fixation on achieving a particular form keeps the practice centred on the ego, locking the mind in a state of restlessness, agitation, and reactivity.

Saitalyam refers to a surrender of preconceived notions regarding the shape of the body or the state of the mind. It involves a shift in focus from exertion to cultivating a sense of contentment (santosha) that arises from knowing we have put in our best efforts. With this contentment, we surrender the outcomes of our efforts to Ishvara, which can be a personal deity or the universe at large. Our focus then shifts from achieving a specific form to experiencing and being absorbed in the energy that moves and supports the body in various postures and illuminates our awareness as well. During these moments, our awareness transcends and becomes aware of awareness itself, resulting in an experience characterised by lightness, expansiveness, freedom, and inner energy.

We are not merely defined by the physical form we inhabit; we are the expression of formless energy that takes shape. In the practice of asana, we embark on a journey to release the tight, vice-like grip of the physical body and the mental projections that often confine us. One of Manoj Kaimal's constant reminders in class is to not to be just fixated on how far back the arm can go, but instead try to sense the energy that moves the arm. It is through this process that we begin to coalesce, to merge (samapattibhyam) our individual existence with the boundless, limitless, and formless essence of the universe, referred to as 'ananta', that which has no beginning and no end.

Thus, we can see that the significance of asana transcends the physical realm. It is not merely about contorting the body into various postures but a deeper exploration of our inner world and the limitless potential that lies within. As we engage in the art of moving meditation, we unravel layers of self, slowly shedding the ego's grasp on rigid shapes and predetermined outcomes.

The journey from form to formless and back again, akin to the wave's graceful return to the ocean, allows us to experience a profound sense of unity. It is in these moments of asana practice that we realise the boundless nature of our existence. This moving meditation not only enhances our physical well-being but also serves as a pathway to connect with the universal essence, ultimately helping us transcend the limitations of the self.

As we get absorbed in our asana practice, we discover the beauty of form and formlessness coexisting in perfect harmony. This is the dance of the universe, a reminder that we are both distinct and connected, individual waves in the vast ocean of consciousness. This realisation opens the door to a deeper understanding of the self and the limitless potential that lies within.

* * *

Practical Exercise

Let's explore asana through the lens of Ashtanga yoga as outlined in the Patanjali Yoga Sutras. This comprehensive examination not only delves into the physical aspects but also the inner dimensions of our practice.

1. **Ahimsa (Non-Violence):** Begin by asking if the principle of non-violence is upheld in your asana practice. Are you respecting your body's limitations and avoiding injury and self-criticism?

2. **Satya (Truthfulness):** Consider whether truthfulness is present in your asana. Are you being honest with yourself about your abilities and challenges in each pose?

3. **Santosha (Contentment):** Reflect on your practice and assess if you experience contentment. Are you

content with where you are in your practice, or do you constantly compare and strive to compete?

4. **Tapas (Effort):** Evaluate the level of effort you put into your practice. Is your effort consistent and disciplined, or does it waver depending on your mood or external circumstances?

5. **Svadhyaya (Self-Study):** Examine whether self-study is an ongoing part of your practice. Do you take time to introspect and learn from your experiences on the mat?

6. **Isvara Pranidhana (Surrender):** Consider if there is the attitude of surrender in your practice. Are you attached to specific outcomes, or can you release the need to control and surrender to the natural flow of your practice?

7. **Pranayama (Breath Regulation):** Pay attention to your breath during asana. Is it calm, steady, and synchronised with your movements, or is it erratic and shallow?

8. **Dharana (Mental Focus):** Determine where your mind is during the practice. Is it fully present in the body and breath, or is it wandering elsewhere, distracted by external thoughts?

9. **Dhyana (Effortless Absorption):** Explore your ability to release efforts and simply be absorbed in the state of the asana. Can you find moments of effortlessness within your practice?

10. **Post-Asana Feeling:** Assess how you feel at the end of your asana session. Do you experience a sense of lightness and renewed energy in both

your body and mind? Does your entire being resonate with joy?

11. **State Shift:** Finally, reflect on whether you have experienced a state shift during your practice. Have you transitioned from a state of restlessness to one of stability, inner harmony and connection?

This comprehensive self-inquiry invites a deeper understanding of your asana practice, helping you align not only with the physical postures but also with the profound principles of Ashtanga yoga, creating a holistic and transformative experience.

❖ **Preparing the Body for Seated Meditation**

Before embarking on breathing and meditation practices, it is essential to prepare your body, particularly your hips, for prolonged sitting. Here are some asanas that can help open and relax your hips and groins, making your experience more comfortable and focused.

❖ **Supta Baddha Konasana**

Supta baddha konasana is a classic hip-opening pose that can be adapted to your hip and groin flexibility level using props like blocks and bolsters. Follow these steps:

• Begin by lying comfortably on your back. For added spinal support, you can place a bolster vertically behind you.

- Bend your knees, keeping the soles of your feet flat on the floor, as close to your hips as possible.
- Let your knees gently open out on either side toward the floor, bringing the soles of your feet together.
- If you feel any inner thigh strain, use blocks to support your outer thighs.
- Allow your arms to rest by your sides.
- Stay in this pose for as long as it feels comfortable, as gravity gradually deepens the stretch.
- Maintain even and steady breathing throughout the posture.
- Feel yourself opening up to receive the healing energy of the universe, embracing a sense of ease (sukham).
- To exit the pose, support your knees as you bring them together, then roll over to one side and sit up.

Start with a short duration, setting a timer for 30 seconds to 1 minute. With regular practice and proper thigh support, you can gradually extend the duration to 3-5 minutes, experiencing the restorative and calming benefits of the posture.

❖ **Seated Kapotasana**
- Begin by sitting with your legs extended straight in front of you.

- Bend your right knee and place your right foot on the left thigh just below the knee.
- Position your hands on the floor behind you to provide support.
- Gradually bend the left knee, bringing your right foot up towards your chest.
- Stop when you encounter any resistance at your right hip or knee, and breathe gently through this sensation.
- Aim to keep the right knee moving away from your chest.
- Work towards closing the gap between your right shin and your chest.
- Sense the opening and release along the right outer hip, keeping your heart open to receive the grace of the universe.
- If you are new to this pose, stay in it for 30 seconds to 1 minute, maintaining steady breathing throughout.
- To exit the pose, straighten the left leg first and then the right.
- Repeat the sequence on the other side.

❖ **Agnistambhasana Variations**

Agnistambhasana, often called fire-log pose due to the feet resembling logs in a fire, involves stacking one foot on top of the other. Each knee lines up directly with the opposite ankle. This position deeply stretches the outer hips, particularly the piriformis muscle, which is frequently responsible for sciatica pain.

- **Variation 1: Adho Mukha Agnistambhasana**

  In this version, you fold forward instead of sitting upright in agnistambhasana. This forward fold intensifies the stretch and hip opening.

- **Variation 2: Parivrtta Agnistambhasana**

  In the second variation, a twist is incorporated into the pose. This variation adds an extra dimension to the stretch.

❖ **Entering Agnistambhasana**

- Start by sitting with your legs extended in front of you.
- Bend your left knee and place your left foot below the right knee, ensuring the left knee and ankle are in a straight line, with the left foot flexed.
- Bend your right knee and position your right foot on the left knee, with the right foot flexed. The right knee will be on top of the left ankle.
- Stack the two shins on top of each other, resembling logs of wood, with both feet flexed.
- Be highly attuned to your hips and knees, avoiding the urge to force a specific outcome.
- Stay in this position, breathing evenly, even through mild discomfort, as this is a practice of titiksha—the capacity to endure discomfort without immediately exiting the pose.

- Spend some time getting comfortable in this position and practising it for a few weeks before attempting the variations.

❖ **Adho Mukha Agnistambhasana (Forward Fold)**

- From the base position, fold forward, transitioning into adho mukha agnistambhasana. You will feel an increased stretch in the outer hips at this stage.
- Maintain mindfulness and adhere to the principles of yamas, such as ahimsa (non-violence) and satya (truth), as you stay in this forward fold. It is also a beautiful gesture of surrender, connecting you to the niyama of ishvara pranidhana. Stay with santosha (contentment).
- Hold this pose for 20-30 seconds, if comfortable.

❖ **Parivrtta Agnistambhasana (Twisted Variation)**

- From agnistambhasana, if you twist to the side with your right elbow against the sole of your right foot, you enter parivrtta agnistambhasana.
- While holding the pose, maintain the twist, with your left palm pressing into your right palm, and your left shoulder and the side of your ribcage twisting back.
- Hold this twist for 20 seconds, breathing evenly and naturally.
- Sense the deep twist along the spine, the opening of the left shoulder and chest, releasing deeply embedded patterns and opening blocked channels of energy.

- Maintain mindfulness and adhere to the principles of yamas, such as ahimsa (non-violence) and satya (truth), as you stay in the twist with santosha (contentment).

- Release the twist and repeat the poses on the other side. You can straighten your legs and release your hips at any point. Always be sensitive to your hips and knees while exploring these poses.

Cale vate calam cittam niscale niscalam bhavet yogi sthanutvamapnoti tato vayum nirodhayet.

(When the breath is agitated, the mind is unsteady. When breath becomes steady, [the mind] also is steady, and the yogin attains steadiness [and stillness]. Hence one should restrain the [agitated] breath.)

—Hathayogapradipika

Chapter 6

PRANAYAMA

Pranayama involves the intentional regulation of both the inhalation and exhalation of breath as well as breath retention. While it's commonly referred to as 'breathing exercises' in common parlance and for the sake of convenience, it is crucial for yoga practitioners to understand that pranayama goes beyond mere breathing techniques. It is the conscious engaging, enhancing, and deepening of our connection to prana, the life force that animates us all.

As practitioners delve deeper into their practice, their focus shifts from the mechanical aspects of breath to the subtle energy that underlies it. This transformation signifies the transition from basic breathing exercises to pranayama. Pranayama thus serves as a bridge between the individual and the universe, allowing for a profound connection. It's important to note that pranayama should be undertaken only after achieving proficiency in asana practice.

Going beyond the processes of inhalation and exhalation is pranayama. Pranayama is not just about breathing deeply, but is rather a state when one transcends the breath itself. We become one with prana, the cosmic catalyst, the universal life force.

— Yogacharya Dr Ananda Balayogi Bavanani,
Understanding the Yoga Darshan

Forming a Connecting with Our Breath

2.49 Tasmin sati svasa prasvasayor gati vicchedah pranayamah.

(That [firm posture] being acquired, the movements of inhalation and exhalation should be regulated. This is pranayama.)

When we think of pranayama, we often visualise a practitioner sitting with closed eyes, dedicating a fixed period each day or perhaps practising once a week in a class setting. However, the scope of pranayama extends far beyond these conventional notions. As our relationship with the breath deepens, it becomes a constant companion in various life situations.

In these everyday scenarios, which might not be conducive to striking a yoga pose, we can always work with the breath to restore some semblance of calm and clarity to our minds. Thus, our body and breath emerge as potent tools for managing our mental states. It is worth noting that while everyone possesses a body and breath, not everyone is aware of how to skillfully utilise them. Yoga practice equips us with the knowledge to guide our minds toward stability and harmony.

And similar to building any relationship in life, whether with a child, a partner, or a job, demands time and attention, nurturing a deep connection with the body and breath requires consistent focus and practise too. Only then does our breath becomes a reliable friend to turn to in trying times. But if we haven't maintained that friendship through regular and diligent practise, its significance may not readily come to mind during moments of crisis.

The process of building this connection is akin to forming a samskara, a deep-seated pattern within us. When adversity strikes, we should instinctively know who to call and how to respond. If our daily practice has become an integral part of our lives, it will equip us to better respond to life's challenges, ultimately shaping the story of our lives. It is in our moment-to-moment responses that our life is shaped. So, the knowledge and ability to work skillfully with our body and breath empowers us to respond to life's trials without succumbing to bitterness, depression, or illness.

Exploring Prana

While the term 'prana' is often used interchangeably with 'breath', it's essential to understand that breath is just one of the conduits through which prana enters our bodies. This universal life force, known as prana in Sanskrit, represents the energy of the cosmos. Energy, in its various forms, has been, currently is, and will always be an intrinsic aspect of our existence. It is the driving force behind all observable movements in the universe and the essence that allows us to function fully as living beings. This universal energy is often referred to as 'vishwa' (universal prana) or 'maha' (great prana).

Prana travels on the breath, and with every inhalation, we beckon the infinite energy and potentiality of the universe. Conversely, each exhalation is an act of releasing our individuality, letting go of our ego and pettiness to merge back into the universe. Our pranayama practice serves as a graceful dance between 'saha' (universal consciousness) and 'aham' (individual consciousness). Through this practice, we bridge our disconnection from the universe and experience a profound sense of empowerment, healing, and wholeness.

Much of our communication with the world occurs at an energetic level. Just as we present ourselves with a physical 'look', we also carry a distinct energetic signature. As we become attuned to the energies within and around us, we start to recognise the vibrational signature that accompanies us in every interaction and endeavour. We also become more sensitive to the energy around us. For example, we can tangibly sense the energy of an angry individual in a room or feel the soothing energy in the environment as we sit on a beach, watching the waves roll in. There is also the subtle energy transmission we experience when we are seated near an evolved teacher

In the realm of Vedanta philosophy, there is a concept known as 'sharira trayam' or the 'three bodies'. According to this philosophy, we extend beyond our physical body (sthula sharira) and possess a subtle energy or astral body (sukshma sharira) as well as a causal seed body (karana sharira). The subtle body is connected through an extensive network of pathways known as 'nadis', which channel the life force throughout the entire body, similar to how blood flows through veins, capillaries, and arteries in our physical body. Various authors have estimated their numbers to range from 72,000 to 350,000.

On a physical level, the nadis correspond to our nervous system. The three most significant nadis are ida, pingala, and sushumna. Prana flows along ida nadi, linked to the left nostril, driven by cooling lunar energy associated with the parasympathetic nervous system. In contrast, prana flows along pingala nadi, connected to the right nostril, driven by the warm solar energy linked to the sympathetic nervous system. Prana flowing through the sushumna nadi, is signified by the balanced flow of energy through the ida and pingala in the subtle body and through both nostrils in the gross body, accompanied by a deeper, stable state of awareness. Minimising ida and pingala flow, causing prana to flow in the sushumna, is an essential preparation for meditation and kundalini awakening.

The presence of prana is evident in every facet of our lives. It is the energy that propels the movement of our thoughts, the rhythm of our respiration, the processes of digestion and circulation. In our homes, one single unified source of electric energy serves various purposes such as heating, cooling, sound, and more, and we label it differently based on its functions. Likewise, the one universal energy, prana, is known by different names too, according to its different functions.

The maha prana enters our bodies with our first breath of life and through the navel energy centre (Manipura chakra), animates the trillions of cells in our body, transforming us into individual living entities. Before our birth, we depended on our mother's life force. However, with our first breath, we become independent individuals, driven by prana. Prana then manifests through different prana vayus: prana (respiration), samana (digestion), udana (communication), vyana (circulation), and apana (elimination). Nevertheless, all of these are merely expressions of the same fundamental life force.

Pancha Vayus

Hrdi prano gude'panah samano nabhi manadale
Udanah kantha desastho vyanah sarva sariragah.
(The seat of prana is in the heart, apana, the anus, samana, the region above the navel, udana, the throat and vyana moves all over the body.)
— Shiva Samhita

As previously discussed, the pancha vayus represent the five vital flows of universal prana within us. These vayus enable our physiological functions, allowing us to function as human beings. Our annamaya kosha, the structural layer of our existence, relies on the flow of prana through us. For example, while the anatomical heart is part of our body's structural makeup, it is the pranamaya kosha, the energy layer of our existence, that animates and sustains it, enabling it to pump blood, supply oxygen, and distribute nutrients throughout the body. While each vayu is associated with a specific area of the body, we must know that their influence isn't confined to a physical location but extends to various functions within the body.

Their subtle energetic movements affect the state of our physical, emotional, and mental health. If vayu becomes imbalanced, it can disrupt the whole energetic system of the body and negatively affect the organs linked to its location. Yogacharya Dr Ananda Balayogi Bhavanani provides an insightful description of the different prana vayus and their functions.

1. Prana Vayu

Responsible for respiration and primarily centred in the heart region (hrdi prano), prana vayu plays a vital role in the entire body. Respiration involves more than the expansion and contraction of the lungs; it encompasses cellular respiration, occurring within every cell, where oxygen breaks down food molecules to generate chemical energy. This process fuels various physical activities, including digestion, muscle movement, and cognitive functions. Prana's energy is characterised by an upward flow, influencing everything that enters our bodies, such as air, food, thoughts, ideas, and impressions. It serves as the foundational energy that governs other energies as well. When balanced, it instils a sense of grounding and optimism, allowing us to view life with a perspective of possibility. Imbalances in prana vayu may lead to cravings, restlessness, anxiety, and low energy. Also, it is associated with the anahata chakra and the element of air.

2. Apana Vayu

Apana vayu is primarily situated at the end of the digestive tract, specifically in the anal region (gude apana). Its energy flows downward and outward, making it responsible for elimination and excretion processes in the body, including the menstrual cycle and childbirth in women.

Apana vayu governs the elimination of waste products generated during metabolic processes, including urine, stool, and carbon dioxide. Sweating, a form of elimination that occurs through the skin's pores, is also associated with apana vayu. Like other vayus, apana's function should be seen holistically, considering all processes, such as cellular waste elimination and respiration. An imbalance in apana vayu can manifest physically as difficulties with elimination and emotionally as an inability to release certain thoughts and memory patterns, leading to emotional distress. It is linked to the muladhara chakra and the element of earth.

3. Samana Vayu

Samana vayu is centred in the navel area (nabhi mandale) and flows from the body's periphery toward its centre. It governs the digestion and assimilation of various substances, including food, air, experiences, emotions, and thoughts. Samana plays a crucial role in what is often referred to as 'mental digestion', enabling us to process and assimilate complex concepts and information. Digestion involves the breakdown of complex substances into simpler forms for easy assimilation. This is true for food, where proteins are broken down into amino acids, as well as for abstract concepts. The ability to digest life experiences and concepts plays a pivotal role in developing a healthy self-esteem and maintaining healthy relationships. An imbalance in samana vayu can lead to physical issues related to absorption and food elimination, as well as mental challenges in processing information rationally. It is associated with the manipura chakra and the element of fire.

4. Udana Vayu

Udana vayu is situated at the throat (kanta deshastu) and supports communication processes. This includes speaking, listening, and non-verbal communication. Udana flows upward from the heart to the head and circulates around the neck, governing speech, self-expression, and growth. An imbalance in udana vayu can lead to speech difficulties, a lack of self-expression, and throat-related diseases. From a holistic perspective, udana vayu is responsible for intra-cellular and inter-cellular communication in the body. It also plays a crucial role in transitions between states of consciousness, including wakefulness, sleep, dreams, and deeper states like samadhi or death. Udana vayu is connected to the vishuddha chakra and the element of ether.

5. Vyana Vayu

Vyana vayu circulates throughout the entire body, flowing from the body's centre to its periphery. It oversees comprehensive bodily energy systems, including the circulatory system, lymphatic system, and the entire nervous system, encompassing sensory and motor functions, as well as the transmission of sensations from the body to the brain and motor commands from the brain to the body.

By working with and learning to consciously control these energy flows, ancient yogis achieved not only optimal health and well-being but also activated the primordial kundalini energy, leading to states of enlightenment.

These explanations of the prana vayus provide an in-depth understanding of the essential roles these energies play in our physical and mental well-being, highlighting their interconnectedness and influence on various bodily functions.

The Breath as a Profound Teacher

When we engage in the practice of observing the breath, we enter into a deep exploration of the universe's nature. Each breath can be likened to a microcosm of life, offering us a profound glimpse into the impermanence of existence mirrored in the constant ebb and flow of the breath. As we come to realise the futility of trying to grasp on to either an inhalation or exhalation, we can reflect on our futile attempts to cling to life itself or coerce particular life situations to endure. This realisation assists us in accepting the inescapable passage of our loved ones and, perhaps, our own mortality when that moment arrives. It also helps us embrace the natural life cycle of many situations we encounter, alleviating our struggle with the greatest source of pain in our lives— our resistance to change.

Indeed, when we contemplate our life's journey, we encounter a plethora of situations that cause us immense suffering: the conclusion of a relationship, divorce, the loss of a spouse, the evolution of our children into independent individuals, the transformation of cherished friendships into sour relationships, or the shift of siblings from allies to adversaries engaged in courtroom battles. It is our incapacity to accept these changes that often inflicts the most intense pain.

Nonetheless, contemplating the innate ebb and flow of life imparts a new perspective, rendering the journey of life far less agonizing. By understanding that life's course follows its own rhythm and that we have limited control over how others respond to us, we begin to navigate these situations more gracefully. The wisdom derived from our focused observation of the breath empowers us to flow with life's currents.

The insights garnered from this practice trigger profound shifts in our perspective. They help us distinguish objective facts from our subjective narratives, stories, and the emotions that fuel them. In doing so, we gain a precious freedom – freedom from the constraints of our self-imposed narratives and the unnecessary suffering they create.

The Influence of Breath on Various Facets of Our Lives

Breath plays a fundamental role in shaping every aspect of our lives, encompassing our mind, body, nervous system, brain, and emotions. It affects the rhythm of our heartbeat, illustrating the profound interconnectedness of our breathing patterns and our identity. Understanding the impact of our breath on our lives is crucial for unlocking our full potential. In the following section, we will delve into how our breath influences various facets of our existence.

- **On the Mind**

  The breath and the mind share an intricate relationship as they are interdependent. Regulating our breath is synonymous with regulating our mind. The breath stands as one of the most potent tools at our disposal to shape the state of our minds and bodies. It empowers us to manage stress and anxiety, reduce blood pressure and heart rate, shift brainwave frequencies, and even alter gene expression. This profound connection between the mind and breath forms the cornerstone of our practice and our good health.

  Cale vate calam cittam niscale niscalam bhavet
  Yogi sthanutvamapnoti tato vayum nirodhayet.

  (When the breath is agitated, the mind is unsteady. When breath becomes steady, [the mind] also is steady, and the Yogin attains steadiness [and stillness]. Hence one should restrain the [agitated] breath.)

— Hatha Yoga Pradipika

• **On the Nervous System**

Ideally, the sympathetic and parasympathetic systems should work in harmony, responding to life events by turning on and off as needed. However, the stresses of modern life continually bombard us from the moment we wake up, which pushes our nervous system into a perpetual fight or flight mode, characterised by a sympathetic overdrive. Being in this state constantly unleashes a surge of stress hormones like cortisol, adrenaline, and noradrenaline into our bloodstream. This phenomenon of chronic stress is now considered the primary cause of many prevalent illnesses. Engaging in a daily pranayama practice has the remarkable effect of stimulating your salivary glands. This leads to an increased production of saliva, a significant indicator of heightened parasympathetic activity, helping our bodies achieve a state of profound relaxation and inner peace. Additionally, through practices such as asana, pranayama, yoga nidra, dharana, and dhyana, we can activate the parasympathetic nervous system and restore balance to our nervous system.

• **On Emotions**

Our breath and emotions are intrinsically intertwined. We all remember being told as children to take deep breaths when experiencing emotional turmoil to regain emotional equilibrium. Scientific research substantiates this, demonstrating that changes in our breathing patterns can directly impact our emotional states. When we are angry and agitated, our breath becomes shallow and irregular. When we are relaxed and contemplative, our breath flows gently and smoothly. By consciously working to regulate our breath patterns through regular pranayama practice, we can deliberately shift our ingrained breathing patterns and their emotional counterparts. Life experiences may trigger anxiety, fear, rigidity, and closure. However, by diligently embracing pranayama, we can remain open, calm, grounded, curious, and creative.

- **On the Brain**

Our brain is a dynamic centre of electrical activity, where neurons communicate through electrical impulses. These electrical signals create brainwaves that vary in frequency, defining our state of consciousness and mental activity. Brainwaves span a spectrum from highly active to less active, with different waves dominating at various times of the day, depending on our activities. By consciously slowing our breathing, we can shift our brainwaves from high beta to alpha. The beta state is where we operate for most of the day, characterised by analytical thinking, planning, and assessment. In the slower alpha state, there is more space between thoughts, enabling us to consciously choose our thought patterns. This promotes states of calmness and peace, creating an environment conducive to significant changes through suggestions, affirmations, and intentions. Similar transitions occur when our brain waves shift from the active beta state to the relaxed alpha state, which typically occurs just before we fall asleep at night. Another opportunity for affirmations arises immediately upon waking in the morning, before the brain waves shift into an active beta state.

The brain's hemispheres are intricately linked to the sides of the body, with the left side connected to the right brain and the right side connected to the left brain. Each hemisphere represents distinct functions, with the left brain associated with logic, calculation, and linear thinking, while the right brain embodies creativity, imagination, and holistic thinking. The ida nadi energy flow, which corresponds to breathing along the left nostril, is linked to the right brain, and the pingala nadi energy flow, which corresponds to breathing along the right nostril, is connected to the left brain. By consciously working with the breath, whether through single or alternate nostril breathing, we can harmonise both hemispheres of the brain, promoting physical and emotional equilibrium.

Pranayama: The Key to Unlock Our Highest Potential

Pranayama holds the key to tapping into the boundless intelligence and energy of the universe. Our ancient yogis were relentless in their pursuit of exploring and expressing the highest aspects of human existence and realised that pranayama provided the gateway to a realm brimming with potential and limitless possibilities.

2.52 Tatah kshiyate prakasha avaranam.
(As its result, the veil over the inner light is destroyed.)

Pranayama kshiyate (destroys) the avaranam (veil) that shrouds our prakasha (inner light). This veil is formed by the impurities that obscure our mind: ignorance, ego, desire, delusion, anger, greed, lust, jealousy, and more. These impurities block our energy and thus cloud our intelligence and clarity. Engaging in pranayama practice allows us to gradually release the blocks on our energy and thus reduce the darkness that conceals our inner wisdom and clarity. These preparatory states are essential as they ready the mind to access deeper levels of concentration and meditation.

Pranayama also plays a pivotal role in releasing toxic patterns that keep us stuck in the past by dissolving blocked energy. In the Yoga Chudamani Upanishad, it is said that there is no discipline higher than pranayama. It is called exalted knowledge (mahavidya), a royal road to well-being, freedom, and bliss. By purifying the mind and body through pranayama, we uncover our innate potential and pave the way for profound transformation, allowing us to access the boundless wisdom and inner clarity that resides within us.

What Constitutes Pranayama Practice?

The phrase 'breath is life' highlights the fundamental connection between conscious existence and the act of breathing. Our life begins with our first breath and concludes with our last. A consistent pranayama practice offers numerous benefits, spanning the physical, physiological, emotional, and spiritual dimensions of our being.

The sutras outline several key components of a pranayama practice. This includes the flow of breath which can be bahya (external), abhyantara (inward), and stambha (pauses). We can also focus (desa) on a specific area like the ribcage, abdomen, etc., for a prescribed duration (kala), like 6:6 or 8:8 counts for inhales and exhales. This process needs to be repeated (samkhyabhih) for a certain number of rounds such as 9 or 18. Maharishi Patanjali also emphasises the importance of a long (dirga) and subtle (sukshmah) breath.

Is Asana a Prerequisite for Pranayama?

Many of us believe that there is nothing wrong with our breathing but if we look closely, we will realise that the majority of us have suboptimal breathing patterns. Our daily habits, such as slouching in front of a computer or hunching over a desk, do not foster optimal breathing. Though it may appear that breathing centres on the nose, the nose serves merely as a portal for air to enter and exit. In the Manasa Yoga tradition, breathing is regarded as a form of movement where the body's posture plays a critical role. Hence, the quality of our breath is intricately linked with our bodily posture.

Both Maharishi Patanjali in the Yoga Sutras and Yogi Svatmarama in the *Hatha Yoga Pradipika* emphasise the importance of asana practice in developing a stable posture, enhancing focus, and gaining control over the mind. Moreover, it facilitates the ability to sit for extended periods without succumbing to restlessness and discomfort. Proper breathing also necessitates open hips and the release of muscles along the hamstrings, adductors, and rectus femoris, creating space for movement within the abdomen and ribcage. Regular asana practice contributes significantly to achieving these prerequisites for effective pranayama.

* * *

Practical Exercises

Pranayama comprises three primary components: inhalation (puraka), exhalation (rechaka), and retention (kumbhaka). It is crucial to understand that when working with the subtle force of prana, one should never force or hold the breath until it becomes uncomfortable. Ideally, you should focus on retention only after consistently practising inhalation and exhalation for a few months. The quality of your breath is deeply interconnected with the state of your mind. Remember, there is no competition or achievement in pranayama; our primary focus should be directed towards cultivating a deep and intimate relationship with our breath, characterised by love, respect, and patience.

❖ Observing Your Natural Breath

Initiating your pranayama journey begins with a simple yet essential step—observing your natural breath. This initial awareness of your breath's flow unveils unconscious emotional, mental, and physical patterns (samskaras). To transform and heal these patterns, you must first recognise them. Otherwise, your breath will continue to reflect your inner experiences, whether it is anxiety, pain, joy, or enthusiasm, while you remain unaware.

❖ **Deergha Swaasam (Extended Breath)**

Once you can consciously direct your attention to your breath and hold it steady for a while, you can progress to the next stage. When you are stressed, your breath tends to be quick and shallow. Deep breathing, on the other hand, facilitates a more significant flow of oxygen to your brain, especially the cortex, making you more alert and energised. You can practice deep breathing anywhere, at any time of the day, whether you are stuck in traffic, in an elevator, or at the office. Here is how to do it:

- Sit comfortably with your eyes closed and your spine upright.
- Exhale deeply, gently drawing your abdomen toward your spine.
- Inhale deeply, expanding your abdomen, lower chest, and upper chest, feeling your collarbones lift and spread.
- Exhale, allowing the collarbones, chest, and abdomen to descend.
- Maintain a continuous flow during both inhalation and exhalation, initially with a count of 6:6.
- Repeat this process up to 6 times to start.
- After three months of practice, you can do Savitri Pranayama by adding both internal and external

breath retention. Start gently, with half the count of your inhalation and exhalation (e.g., 6:3:6:3).

- So, inhale to a count of 6, hold for a count of 3 (internal retention), exhale to a count of 6, and hold for a count of 3 (external retention). Focus on slow, deep and rhythmic breathing.

Pay attention to the flow of your breath as you move away from deliberate deep breathing. Observe how your breath naturally settles, notice the shift in your mental state, the settling of energy, and the ease (sukham) that permeates your entire being. Don't be in a hurry to open your eyes or move. The purpose of this practice is to access deeper dimensions within ourselves, which often remain inaccessible amidst the stresses of daily life.

❖ Ujjayi Pranayama (Victorious Breath)

Ujjayi, meaning 'victorious', is a breath often used during asana (posture) practice, particularly in Ashtanga vinyasa classes. It involves making a soft hissing sound by directing your inhales and exhales over the back of your throat. Ujjayi promotes full lung expansion and has a calming effect on your mind. Here is how to practice Ujjayi:

- Sit comfortably with your spine tall and aligned.
- Keep your eyes closed and focus on your breath.
- Inhale deeply through your nose.

- At the beginning, exhale slowly, with your mouth open as if you were about to whisper a secret, creating a 'haaaaaaaah' sound.
- Concentrate on maintaining long inhales and exhales, ideally with an even count like 6:6.
- Place your attention on the sound and sensation of your breath at the back of your throat.
- As you begin the practice, both inhalation and exhalation can be with the mouth open, but once you are comfortable, the practice should be done with your mouth closed.
- After about a month of regular practice, begin to incorporate internal and external breath retention. Start gently, again with half the count of your inhalation and exhalation (e.g., 6:3:6:3).
- So, inhale to a count of 6, hold for a count of 3 (internal retention), exhale to a count of 6, and hold for a count of 3 (external retention).
- Repeat 6-9 times.

Maintain your attention on your breath after you finish the deliberate breathing. Feel the shift in your breath pattern, the state of your mind, the lightness of your body, and the settling of your energy and experience the ease (sukham) within you. Don't be in a hurry to open your eyes or move. The purpose of this practice is to access deeper dimensions within ourselves, which often remain inaccessible amidst the stresses of daily life.

❖ Bhramari Pranayama (Bee's Breath)

Bhramari pranayama gets its name from the Indian black bee called Bhramari, as it mimics the soothing humming sound vibrations created by a bee. This provides instant relief from stress and helps alleviate agitation, frustration, and anxiety. It also enhances various body functions, including lung function and immunity. Here is how to practice Bhramari:

- Sit comfortably with your spine tall and aligned.
- Close your eyes and focus on your breath.
- Inhale deeply through your nose.
- Gently press your eardrums with your index fingers and exhale as long as you can with a loud, high-pitched hum.
- Begin with 6 repetitions.

After your practice, sit quietly for a few moments to absorb the vibrations' residue, both inside and outside of you. Observe the sensations in your body, the calmness and peace within, the shift in your mental state, and the energy that fills you with bliss (ananda). Don't be in a hurry to open your eyes or move. The purpose of this practice is to access deeper dimensions within ourselves, which often remain inaccessible amidst the stresses of daily life.

❖ Nadi Shodhana/Anuloma Viloma

Nadi Shodhana, also known as nerve purification or alternate nostril breathing, is a potent and calming pranayama practice that activates the parasympathetic nervous system. By focusing on long exhalations, which are twice the duration of inhalations, it helps cleanse and de-stress. This technique is especially effective when you are anxious, nervous, feeling imbalanced, or having trouble falling asleep. Here is how to practice it:

- Sit comfortably with your eyes closed, maintaining an upright and aligned spine.
- Begin with a few even breaths.
- Form a fist with your right hand, extending your thumb and last two fingers while keeping the middle fingers tucked into your palm.
- Close your right nostril with your right thumb and exhale fully. Then inhale through your left nostril.
- Close your left nostril with the ring finger of your right hand, release the thumb, and exhale slowly through your right nostril. Ensure the exhalation is twice as long as the inhalation.
- Inhale through your right nostril.
- Close your right nostril with your right thumb and exhale through your left nostril. Inhale again through your left nostril.
- Repeat these cycles, alternating between right and left nostrils.
- As the exhalation is twice the length of the inhalation (1:2), if you inhale for four counts, exhale for eight counts, and so on. You can incorporate breath retention into the practice later on, but only

after regularly practising the basic technique for at least three months.

- A suitable ratio for retention for beginners is 1:1:2:1 (e.g., inhale for four counts, retain for four counts, exhale for eight counts, and retain after exhalation for another four counts).

- A traditional ratio is 1:4:2:4, which means inhaling for four counts, retaining for sixteen counts, exhaling for eight counts, and retaining after exhalation for another sixteen counts. However, it's recommended to progress gradually with retention practice. The quality of your exhalations is crucial, and they should always be soft and subtle. Rushed or uneven exhalations indicate forced retention. Build your capacity for retention slowly, keeping in mind the interconnectedness of the mind, body, and breath.

- Start with six cycles, and once you have completed the practice, take a moment to experience the soothing energies awakened in your body and mind.

As you continue to observe your breath, it will become increasingly subtle, to the point where you might feel as though you are hardly breathing. Your mind will also reach a quiet, open, and spacious state, with minimal mental activity, such as thoughts, opinions, and judgments. This is the state of inner peace and joy you seek, which can only be found within you, and this is the reason why you must persist with these practices.

❖ Chakra Pranayama

Chakra, which means 'wheel', refers to the energy centres in our body used as focal points in various meditation practices. These energy vortices spiral around the Sushumna nadi, the central energy channel, extending into higher dimensions. They act as transformers channelling universal energy into our bodies.

Chakras are also closely linked to endocrine glands, major organs, and massive nerve centres. Each chakra holds beliefs, emotions, and memories associated with specific areas of our lives, influencing our physical, psychological, emotional, and spiritual well-being.

While the exact number of chakras is not known, we know that they exist in our subtle body. Here are the seven main chakras, each with its corresponding colour:

1. Muladhara chakra (Root chakra) - Red

2. Swadhisthana chakra (Sacral chakra) - Orange

3. Manipura chakra (Solar plexus chakra) - Yellow

4. Anahata chakra (Heart chakra) - Green

5. Vishuddhi chakra (Throat chakra) - Blue

6. Ajna chakra (Third-eye chakra) - Indigo

7. Sahasrara Chakra (Crown chakra) - Violet

Now we will explore how to practise Chakra Pranayama:

- Sit comfortably in a cross-legged position, close your eyes, and maintain an upright and aligned spine.
- Exhale completely, then inhale (6 counts), feeling the energy flow upwards through the sushumna nadi (which corresponds with the spine in the gross body) from the Muladhara chakra to the Ajna chakra, following the colours of the rainbow (VIBGYOR).
- As you exhale (6 counts), feel the energy flow down the spine, from the Ajna chakra to the Muladhara chakra.
- Continue this flow for nine rounds.
- After a few months of practice, incorporate both internal and external breath retention. Start gently, with half the count of your inhalation and exhalation (6:3:6:3).
- Inhale to a count of 6, hold for 3 counts (internal retention), exhale for 6 counts, and hold for another 3 counts (external retention).
- To enhance the practice, vividly visualise the colours of each chakra as your awareness and breath seamlessly flow up and down the chakras.
- Complete 6 rounds of this practice.

At the end of the chakra pranayama, bring your energy and attention to the space just above the top of your head, where the Sahasrara chakra (the 'thousand-petaled lotus') resides. Visualise and hold steady the beautiful image of the thousand petals of the lotus in vibrant hues of violet. Connect to universal energies that open up to you. Revel in the intertwining of energy between individual consciousness and universal consciousness. Release even the awareness of the breath. Simply be.

Don't be in a hurry to open your eyes or move. The purpose of this practice is to access deeper dimensions within ourselves, which often remain inaccessible amidst the stresses of daily life.

Tasmad yasya maha-baho nigrihitani sarvashah
Indriyanindriyarthebhyas tasya prajna
pratishthita.

(Therefore, one who has restrained the senses
from their objects, O mighty armed Arjun, is
firmly established in transcendental knowledge.)

—The Bhagavad Gita

Chapter 7

Pratyahara

Pratyahara: The Inward Journey

Pratyahara, the fifth limb of Ashtanga yoga detailed in the Yoga Sutras by Maharishi Patanjali, signifies a profound turning inward—a reorientation toward the self. It plays a pivotal role in paving the way for the higher limbs of yoga, including dharana (concentration) and dhyana (meditation), to flourish. The essence of pratyahara revolves around understanding the relationship between our attention and the external sensory world, governed by the fundamental principle 'yatho mana tatah prana' which signifies that wherever the mind wanders, energy follows. So, if our attention is always ensnared by the varied sense objects of the external world, our energy too will be scattered and restless.

From Indriya Jala to Indriya Jaya: The Journey of Transcendence

To turn our focus inward, we must disentangle ourselves from the relentless allure of sensory distractions. So, how can we achieve this shift? Pratyahara is a deeply internal process that doesn't require physically blocking the indriyas, which encompasses the five jnana (perception) indriyas and five karma (action) indriyas, such as closing our eyes or ears. Instead, it entails an internal redirection of our attention.

The mind, often referred to as the 'ekendriya' or the super sense, serves as the central force behind all other senses. It acts as the energy source for the entire sensory system. While there are ten primary senses in total, all of them are ultimately subservient to the mind, collectively forming what is sometimes termed as the eleven senses. The jnana indriyas—comprising the eyes, ears, nose, tongue, and skin—act as conduits through which the mind receives information from the external world. On the other hand, the karma indriyas—encompassing the mouth, hands, feet, and the organs of reproduction and excretion—enable us to respond to and express ourselves in that world.

The transformative power of pratyahara resides within the ajna chakra, situated in the prefrontal cortex of the brain. This is where our capacity to choose, driven by a robust intellect, allows us to harness control over the mind. It marks a profound evolutionary shift, moving us from mere reaction to thoughtful response, from instinctual behaviour to intuitive discernment, and from reflexive actions to reflective engagement.

Through consistent pratyahara practice, we transition from a scattered state of attention to one that is focused and purposeful. It necessitates an ongoing, moment-to-moment practice of consciously redirecting our attention whenever we feel the compulsion to chase after external sense objects. This steady effort ultimately leads us to attain 'jaya', a victory over the influence of the senses.

2.54 Svavisaya asamprayoge cittasya svarupanukarah iva indriyanam pratyaharah.
(Organs of action and perception [indriyanam], when their contact is lost [asamprayoge] with their respective objects [sva vishaya], they then follow [anukara] the individual consciousness [chitta], towards its true nature [svarupa].)

— Patanjali Yoga Sutras

It is fascinating to observe that each of our sensory organs is inherently drawn to specific objects of desire, known as 'sva vishaya'. The eyes are naturally inclined towards the beauty of forms, and they might even fixate on a particular form. The ears crave delightful sounds, the tongue yearns for delectable tastes, the skin seeks sensual touches, and the nose follows sweet fragrances. In a sense, we can consider these sensory experiences as a form of 'ahara' (nourishment) and in our ordinary, unconscious way of living, these experiences consume not just our senses but also our mind and intellect.

The external world is teeming with captivating and often mesmerising attractions: where to travel next, which restaurant to dine in, what's the latest branded handbag to acquire, where to strike the next lucrative business deal, or which spa to visit. We may even find ourselves drawn towards certain people, desiring closeness with some while trying to avoid others. In this scenario, our minds and senses become ensnared, much like fish caught in a net (referred to as 'jala') of worldly enticements.

These sensory attractions consistently prompt our senses to oscillate between being drawn toward certain objects and repelled by others. The messages from our senses are relayed to the mind, giving rise to a state of 'kshipta', marked by inner agitation and restlessness. Interestingly, even in the absence of external objects, when we may find ourselves in seclusion, our senses tend to conjure their own internal objects of attraction. This is because our inner mental inclinations, referred to as 'vasanas', act as an inner driving force and propel us towards various desires. Thus, we are all entangled in a similar net of thoughts and reactive responses to people, events, and circumstances.

This net of matter, known as prakriti, extends broadly in the external world and also deeply within us. It clutches at us, much like the tentacles of an octopus and pulls us into its murky depths. Consequently, the mind is always reacting to the senses and being helplessly tossed between polarities such as pleasure and pain, gain and loss, love and hate, etc.

Many individuals spend their entire lives fervently pursuing love, or perhaps indulging in the pursuit of wealth, status, and power, or even seeking fame and adulation. Yet, their journeys often lead to a dark spiral of depression and anxiety. This is because everything they hold dear can vanish in the blink of an eye: the great love of their life, the riches they sacrificed their family and health for, and even the friends they assumed would always stand by them. And as time passes, they are left pondering the true meaning of their lives and whether they squandered their existence chasing futile things. And this entire cycle began with the initial pursuit of a sensory object.

The energies of our sensory organs are deeply intertwined with the mind. When the tongue craves something delicious, the mind follows suit, insisting, 'I must savour that immediately.' A weak intellect, or buddhi, becomes so overpowered by the mind and senses that its discernment dwindles. At this stage, the intellect merely devises strategies for acquiring the desired object as rapidly as possible, often disregarding standards of morality, decency, and fair-play.

Drawing from the wisdom found in the Srimad Bhagavatam, one of Hinduism's revered puranas, we understand that fulfilling the desires of the senses doesn't extinguish them. This process is akin to offering oblations of butter in a fire, which doesn't quench the flames but rather intensifies them. While momentary satisfaction may bring relief, desire resurfaces with even greater force. The mind and senses continually generate a multitude of desires in the pursuit of happiness, and as long as we remain entangled in the game of fulfilling these desires, true happiness remains elusive, much like a mirage on the horizon.

Turtle Wisdom

2.58 Yada sanharate chayam kurmo nganiva sarvashah
Indriyanindriyarthebhyas tasya prajna pratishthita.
(One who is able to withdraw the senses from the

objects, just as a tortoise withdraws its limbs into its shell, is established in divine wisdom.)

— The Bhagavad Gita

The Bhagavad Gita beautifully illustrates the practice of pratyahara using the metaphor of a turtle. Just as a turtle withdraws its head and limbs under its protective shell when it senses danger, we too must seek refuge in the teachings and retract our senses from the sense of objects when it tends to become overly enmeshed in the world of external objects and their affairs. Often, we become overly fixated and compulsive about various aspects of life, such as relationships, social status, or wealth. These obsessions can lead to overwhelming situations where we are unable to eat, sleep, or function, and it can lead to anxiety, depression, and even more dire consequences. During such times, the wisdom of the turtle serves as a reminder of our inner power to draw back our compulsive attention from the sense object and consciously redirect it by choosing another point of focus.

Need for Pratyahara

Pratyahara practice is essential at various points in our lives to prevent us from losing ourselves in the captivating allure of the external world. This practice doesn't imply that we should abstain from pursuing relationships or making a living. Rather, it encourages us to engage in these pursuits from a place of self-connection, rather than from a state of obsession or compulsion that makes it difficult to return to our core being.

In the context of Advaita Vedanta philosophy, we are meant to be one with the universal energy, granting us access to boundless energy. However, under the veil of illusion or 'maya', everything appears limited, including our energy and time. So, we must be discerning about how we allocate our finite units of time and energy. It is important to direct our attention towards profound teachings and healthful pursuits rather than squandering it on trivial distractions like entertainment or excessive social media use. If our attention and energy are continually dissipated by such activities, we may not have access to them when we need to invest them in intensive practices, such as extended meditation or challenging physical exercises.

The necessity of pratyahara can be likened to that of an archer. To hit a target successfully, an archer must first draw the arrow backwards, aligning with the pratyahara practice of withdrawing the mind and senses from their incessant outward pursuits. Only through this withdrawal can the mind's energy be focused and unleashed, with its full potency, toward a specific goal or target. Therefore, the practice of pratyahara is fundamental for achieving success in any field, whether as a top-level athlete, a creative artist, or an entrepreneur.

The Process of Pratyahara

In the practice of pratyahara, we redirect the flow of our outward-bound energy. This involves the intellect making a conscious decision, for example, to refrain from checking social media for a specific duration, such as a couple of hours. Typically, our minds are drawn to seek entertainment, which often involves various stimuli like compelling stories, captivating visuals, and sensory pleasures.

However, when the intellect takes charge and restrains the mind from indulging in these sensory stimulations, the mind gradually begins to settle within itself. During this period of restraint, as the mind receives fewer external sensory inputs, it starts to find contentment in its own intrinsic qualities. Consequently, the mind takes a respite from its habitual patterns of liking, disliking, preferring, and judging various stimuli. This shift in focus also allows the mind to create a space where it can become attuned to new sensations, ultimately deriving joy from its internal experiences. The mind starts to relish the natural rhythm of the body, the graceful flow of the breath, and the expansiveness of the mind itself. This transformation marks the beginning of a profound and intimate connection with the self, often described as a 'divine romance'.

The Need for Pratyahara

Pratyahara offers invaluable support in two significant aspects of our lives:

1. **Inner Dialogue**

    The dialogue we maintain with ourselves is profoundly influential; it shapes the condition of our minds, bodies, and ultimately, our entire existence. On any given day, we produce an astonishing number of thoughts, estimated to be between 60,000 to 70,000, with a staggering 90 per cent of these thoughts being repetitive. This continuous cycle connects our thoughts to the overall state of our lives. It is a reciprocal process: recurring thoughts lead to similar choices, which, in turn, drive our behaviours and experiences, ultimately affecting our emotions. These emotions, in return, reinforce the very same thoughts, perpetuating an unceasing cycle. Thus, our biology, neurocircuitry, neurochemistry, neurohormones, and even genetic expression are intimately linked to our thought processes, actions, and emotional states.

A fundamental principle in neuroscience is that neurons that fire together, wire together, i.e., our nerve cells, forge connections when they fire together frequently. So, if we consistently engage in repetitive thought patterns, make the same choices, and display the same behaviours, we hardwire our brains to operate within established, unconscious habits, and automatic emotional responses. Essentially, if we exist without mindfulness, we function solely based on subconscious programs. Pratyahara plays a crucial role in this context, as it restrains the mind from pursuing unproductive, repetitive thought patterns, empowering us to create more constructive mental habits.

Through pratyahara, we gain the power to avoid a life dominated by constant distraction. Instead, we redirect our scattered focus and energy towards building a purposeful life centred on the things that genuinely matter: enhancing our concentration, doing passionate work, being self-aware and fully present for the people in our lives, and ultimately becoming the best versions of ourselves.

2. Anatomy of an Experience

Every emotionally charged experience leaves a residual energy that settles within our subconscious as patterns and subtle impressions, known as samskaras and vasanas. These samskaras and vasanas unconsciously influence our preferences, inclinations, and skills. Each experience leaves behind a pratyaya, a potentiality of a future experience. According to Maharishi Patanjali, at any given moment, we hold thousands of these potential experiences, or pratyayas.

Whatever we direct our focus towards becomes a vritti, which is our emergent experience of the moment. If we live mindlessly and fail to exercise our capacity to choose a vritti, the predominant elements in our minds—such as worry, anxiety, fear, and confusion—seize control and lead us down a distressing path. This is where the practice of pratyahara steps in. It allows the intellect to consciously intervene, preventing the mind from being engulfed in a detrimental cycle of thought, and instead, opt for a more neutral and less damaging mental direction and be fully present in the task you are currently engaged in.

Before delving into the stages of dharana (concentration), dhyana (meditation), and samadhi (absorption), it is essential to gain awareness of our ongoing thoughts, actions, and emotions. We must refine our pratyahara practice, which involves the skill of withdrawing from negative, repetitive thought patterns and preserving our energy from restless outward dispersion. By diligently applying this practice throughout the day, we can cultivate the ability to consciously disengage from unproductive distractions that occupy the mind, such as work-related concerns, relationship issues, financial worries, or health problems. This sets the stage for a more focused meditation practice, allowing us to concentrate on a single point of attention, like the breath.

* * *

Practical Exercises

❖ **Prepare for Practice**

- Find a comfortable seated position and gently close your eyes while ensuring your spine is tall.
- Take a moment to inquire, 'Where is your mind right now?' Is it preoccupied with work, children, shopping, financial concerns, or self-doubt?
- Consciously shift your focus and energy away from whatever was occupying your mind, directing it to different points in your body: your feet, sit bones, spine, shoulders, arms, neck, and face.

- Begin to tune into your breath and allow your mind to flow with its rhythm.
- In this way, we reverse the outward flow of attention and energy and redirect it towards our physical body and breath, re-establishing a connection with ourselves.
- Take pleasure in this newfound connection with your body and breath. Remember that it is from the known dimensions of ourselves that we move into the unknown.
- Make this exercise a part of your daily practice, particularly at the start of each session to strengthen your inner connection.

❖ **Methods to Conserve Energy**

- Reduce restlessness and fidgeting during your pranayama and asana practices, allowing you to preserve energy.
- Limit the time spent on social media and idle gossip.
- Decrease the frequency of habitual phone-checking every few minutes by establishing phone-free times or zones in your daily routine. Dedicate an hour every morning and evening to not checking your phone, and commit to leaving your phone aside while at the gym, yoga class, or during walks or hikes.
- Cut down on extended periods spent watching news, television series, or movies, which often

inundate the mind with negative impressions of violence and mindless drama.

- Be mindful of the time spent in social interactions that lack depth or purpose, such as meaningless conversations or unproductive arguments.

- Practice withdrawing from excessive mental analysis and debate over past conversations, allowing your mind to find peace once a conversation has concluded.

- Experiment with fasting for 24 hours once a week to withdraw from the need for regular food.

- Challenge your body's craving for comfort by taking cold showers a few times a week.

Yato yato nishcharati manash chanchalam asthiram
Tatas tato niyamyaitad atmanyeva vasham nayet.

(From whatever and wherever the restless mind
wanders, due to its flickering and unsteady nature,
one should withdraw it and bring it back under the
control of the self.)

—The Bhagavad Gita

Chapter 8

DHARANA

Dharana, the sixth limb of yoga, is a profound practice that delves into the essence of concentration and mental focus. Building upon the foundation of yama (ethical principles) and niyama (personal observances), asanas (physical postures), pranayama (breath control), and pratyahara (withdrawal of the senses), dharana marks the yogic journey's ascent into the more refined domains of consciousness.

In the Bhagavad Gita, the nature of the mind has been described as cancala (fickle) and asthira (restless). So, at its core, dharana involves channeling the scattered and distracted mind to cultivate concentration on a single point or object, whether external or internal. This point of focus is often chosen deliberately to cultivate specific mental attributes, such as clarity, purity, or devotion.

As the precursor to dhyana (meditation) and ultimately, samadhi (absorption), dharana is the all-important process that disciplines the wandering mind into a state of focus by transcending the mind's ceaseless chatter.

Flow of the Angas

In the seamless progression of the yogic journey, it is crucial to understand how the various limbs or angas harmoniously come together to allow us to access higher states of consciousness like dharana, dhyana and samadhi.

A conscious life, marked by moment-to-moment awareness of our thoughts, emotions, sensations, actions and surroundings, lays the ground for cultivating dharana. It is by being in the present moment, the now (atha) that we can perceive the intricate beauty and depth of life; from the gentle touch of our fingers on a keyboard to the rhythmic flow of breath to the breeze caressing our cheek. And the asana practice plays a pivotal role in deepening our awareness by directing us to connect with our bodies, breath, thought and emotions.

Pranayama, through the regulation of our breath and energy, then creates an ideal mental environment for concentration to take root.

Pratyahara, the next limb involves the conscious withdrawal of our scattered attention and energy from the external world and its myriad distractions. As long as our minds remain ensnared by sensory objects, concentration remains an elusive goal, as we are trapped in a cycle of ceaseless distractions. This vital practice is akin to the journey of a river winding back to its source, gradually regaining focus and clarity, paving the way for deeper states of meditation.

Dharana, concentration, is intrinsically connected to

dhyana, meditation, as it is the gateway to dhyana. This transition from dharana to dhyana is subtle yet profound, marking the evolution from cultivating intermittent concentration to a state of effortless attention. In this seamless flow of the yoga angas, we embark on a journey that transcends the surface level of existence and delves into the profound realms of the mind and spirit.

Objects of Concentration

In the realm of concentration, the objects of focus can be either external and internal. Externally, one might choose to concentrate on an image of a deity, a captivating painting, or a mandala symbol. The focus can also turn inward, exploring the subtleties of the breath, specific areas within the body like the energy centres (chakras), chanting of mantras or engaging in drishti, where the gaze is directed towards a particular focal point.

3.1 Desha bandha chittasya dharana.
(Locking of consciousness on a chosen object, at a certain place is the practice of concentration.)
— Patanjali Yoga Sutras

However, it is imperative that we approach the chosen object of concentration with a deep sense of reverence, intent, and perhaps even a degree of intimacy. Without profound respect for the practice and process, and deep value to cultivate connection, the requisite energy for developing concentration on the chosen focal point may remain elusive. For instance, when we embark on the practice of observing the breath, mere indifference or boredom won't suffice. A profound relationship with the breath based on deep interest and curiosity must be forged if concentration is to effortlessly happen.

Similarly, developing an intimate connection with life itself is vital. This involves perceiving life not merely as a series of dry concepts and targets but as a tapestry of felt sensations. Take, for example, your hand. It is not just a complex integration of fingers, skin, and 27 finger bones. Yet, by listing these facts in a clinical manner, we fail to forge an intimate connection with the hand. However, when you extend your fingers and deliberately tune into the vibrant energy coursing through them, then clench your fist and gently release it, you can establish a profound connection with the tactile sensation, essentially capturing the essence of your hand. Similarly, to truly appreciate and connect with life and our breath, we must learn to perceive it through the prism of sensation and enrich our experience by transcending the realm of mere abstraction.

Our practice of concentration, dharana, should be carried out with profound respect and dedication (satkara). It is a sacred endeavour in service (asevita) of nurturing the growth of the inherent capacity for unwavering focus. So, whether it unfolds over a span of 45 minutes or a brief 10-minute session, the practices holds intrinsic value, and must be underpinned by deep reverence, recognising it as a sacred path to inner transformation.

These principles play a pivotal role in fostering the development of stable attention. It is through this stability that tranquility emerges, giving rise to the wisdom-bestowing power of concentration—dharana. This journey towards concentration, as guided by Maharishi Patanjali, entails the twin practices of abhyasa (effort) and vairagya (detachment). Just like the two wings of a bird, both are essential for the cultivation of steadfast concentration.

Through sthitau yatnam, the unwavering effort invested over a prolonged and uninterrupted period of time (dirgha kala nairantarya), our attention finds a secure footing—a firm foundation known as drdha bhumih. From this stable ground, the sought-after concentration naturally blossoms. This intertwining of reverence, effort, and detachment paves the path to the pinnacle of dharana, guiding practitioners to a profound state of focused and tranquil awareness.

Exploring Vairagya

A crucial element in nurturing our concentration on the chosen object of attention is the transition from 'reaction to' the present moment to 'relation with' it. Often, we find ourselves entangled in reactionary patterns, wherein our interactions with the present are predetermined by expectations and rigid perspectives. To truly be 'in relation with' the present moment, we must foster a sense of vast accommodation and unconditional acceptance. This quality of an expansive heart, characterised by equanimity (upekshanam), is instrumental in establishing a genuine relationship with our object of concentration.

Another aspect is the development of vairagya, or detachment. It involves letting go of the idea that we should engage in meditation practices only when we are in a state of inner peace. Instead, we should be willing to sit for meditation even during periods of anger, restlessness, sleepiness, frustration, or anxiety. By practising meditation in these varying states, we nurture a profound sense of vairagya—an extensive, all-encompassing detachment.

It is important to distinguish this concept of detachment from its monastic interpretation, which involves refraining from close interactions with the opposite sex. Here, our aim is not to detach from the objects or people themselves but rather from the attachments and aversions we project onto them. This process leads us towards a relational perspective grounded in equanimity and detachment.

Picture the first time you navigate an uncharted trail; there is no established path, and your progress is laboriously slow. However, with each subsequent hike on the same trail, a distinct path begins to emerge. Similarly, when you initially sit down to observe your breath, your mind is riddled with distractions. Yet, it is crucial to recognise that every time you redirect your mind to the breath, you reinforce neural pathways in the brain.

Consider this reinforcement like the way you use weights at the gym to fortify your muscles. Concentration practices such as breath observation and mantra repetition serve to bolster your brain's focus muscles. During your practice sessions, each instance you realise your mind has strayed and gently bring it back to the breath, it is akin to doing a mental bicep curl. Over time, this continual practice strengthens your 'focus muscle' significantly.

Overall, cultivating dharana is an ongoing endeavour. We must guide our minds to stay present in each unfolding moment throughout the day. When we allocate time for our 20-minute practice, maintaining focus becomes more effortless.

Arjuna and Ekagra

In conclusion, by cultivating a relational perspective, nurturing equanimity, and embracing detachment in our meditation practice, we are better equipped to develop unwavering concentration on our chosen object. This shift in our approach fosters a profound connection with the present moment and allows us to engage with life's ever-changing experiences with an expansive and peaceful heart.

In Indian mythology, there exists a legendary tale that vividly illustrates the concept of ekagra or one-pointed concentration. This story revolves around the prominent character of Arjuna, a prince of the Pandava clan and a central figure in the epic Mahabharata. During his youth, Arjuna received a remarkable challenge from his illustrious teacher, Dronacharya, in which he was called to shoot the eye of a wooden sparrow that had been placed on the branches of a tree. All the other princely students too were summoned to take part.

The story goes that Dronacharya then asked them all what they saw. Their responses were diverse and scattered, encompassing the bird, the branches, the tree, the sky, clouds, the sun, and more. However, it was Arjuna's response that set him apart. He declared, 'I see blackness.' Intriguingly, when probed about the nature of this blackness, Arjuna replied, 'It is the blackness at the centre of the sparrow's eye. I see nothing else.'

Arjuna's remarkable ability to maintain unwavering focus on the tiny, obscure target, excluding all distractions, instantly set him apart as an unparalleled archer. His incredible one-pointed concentration enabled him to hit the mark with unparalleled precision.

This story highlights the profound power of ekagra, emphasising the ability to maintain laser-like concentration on a single objective while disregarding all other distractions, which proved to be the key to Arjuna's unmatched archery skills. It underscores the importance of singular dedication and focus in achieving extraordinary mastery.

* * *

Practical Exercises

❖ **Trataka Meditation**

Trataka, meaning 'to see' or 'gaze', is a technique originally rooted in yoga's purification practices, known as shatkarmas. It cleanses the eyes as well as clears the mind of distractions thereby enhancing focus and concentration. This technique is also beneficial for strengthening the eye muscles. Trataka involves maintaining a steady gaze on a candle or lamp's flame without blinking for as long as possible, though other objects like a dot on the wall, a deity, or a flower can also serve as points of focus.

Here is a step-by-step guide to practising Trataka meditation:

- Begin by sitting in a comfortable position with your spine upright.
- Place a lit candle or lamp in front of you at approximately eye level.
- Close your eyes and take a moment to settle into the present moment.
- Bring your awareness to your breath, feeling it flow in and out. This helps release any tension held in your body.
- At this point, set a sankalpa, a resolve, to maintain your focus throughout the practice. Sankalpas activate your willpower, which is the driving force of life.
- Gaze at the flame, allowing the image of the flame to fill your mind.
- Keep your gaze steady, attempting not to blink for as long as possible.
- When thoughts arise, acknowledge them and gently return your attention to the flame.
- As you persist in maintaining a steady gaze, you will notice a reduction in the onslaught of thoughts, leading to a state of stable attention.
- Eventually, your eyes may start to water, and tears may flow. This serves as a form of cleansing. When this happens, close your eyes but continue to hold

the image of the flame in your mind for as long as you can.

- Sense the settled, calm state of your mind as an aftertaste of the practice.
- Open your eyes and repeat the process.

Initially, it may be challenging to sustain the gaze for an extended period, so you can begin with shorter intervals, such as 30 seconds of gazing followed by 30 seconds of rest with your eyes closed, and repeat this pattern for six rounds. Even during the rest periods with your eyes closed, maintain your attention on the object of focus. As you progress, work towards gazing for two minutes and then resting with your eyes closed for two minutes. With five rounds, this approach leads to a deep 20-minute meditation session.

Trataka meditation, with its intense focus on a single object, helps to train the mind in one-pointed concentration and paves the way for dhyana (meditation).

❖ **Breath Dharana**

- Allocate 20 minutes each day to sit in a serene environment where you won't be interrupted.
- Sit in a comfortable cross-legged position with your eyes closed and your spine upright.
- Direct your attention to your breath, maintaining its stability.
- As your mind begins to take pleasure in the sensation of the breath, focusing becomes a less strenuous endeavour.

- A sense of calmness gradually emerges from this centred awareness.

- Out of this calm foundation, a state of concentration starts to evolve.

- At this stage, attention may still occasionally wander, necessitating the setting of sankalpas and a conscious effort to redirect your focus to the breath.

- It is crucial to recognise that calmness and centredness are essential prerequisites for dharana. In the context of yoga, agitation and concentration cannot coexist.

❖ **Chakra Dharana with Petals**

Set aside time for Chakra Dharana, a practice that centres attention on various chakras and their associated petals:

- Sit comfortably in a cross-legged position with your eyes closed and your spine straight.

- Focus your attention on each chakra and visualize its form along with the number of petals it possesses. Take time to hold your attention at each chakra, exploring the space, sensing the energy, and visualizing the petals and their colours.

- Begin by slowly ascending from 1 to 7, then return down for one round. Maintain unhurried attention at each centre.

1. Muladhara chakra (Root chakra): 4 petals
2. Swadhisthana chakra (Sacral chakra): 6 petals
3. Manipura chakra (Solar Plexus chakra): 10 petals
4. Anahata chakra (Heart chakra): 12 petals
5. Vishuddhi chakra (Throat chakra): 16 petals
6. Ajna chakra (Third eye chakra): 2 petals
7. Sahasrara Chakra (Crown chakra): 1000 petals

Conduct this practice to foster deeper concentration and energy awareness, aiding in the journey toward dharana and meditative bliss.

Yatha dipo nivatastho nengate sopama smrta
Yogino yatacittasya yunjato yogam atmanah.

(Just as a flame in a windless place does not
flicker, similarly a yogi holds the inner lamp of
attention steady in meditation.)

—The Bhagavad Gita

Chapter 9

DHYANA

Dhyana meditation, the seventh limb of Ashtanga yoga according to the Yoga Sutras, derives its name from the combination of 'dhi', signifying attention, and 'ayanam', suggesting journey or movement. In essence, meditation is the journey of attention from scattered distractions (kshipta) toward a state of one-pointed focus (ekagra).

Dhyana, as a practice, is intricately connected to the foundations laid by the preceding six limbs: yamas, niyamas, asana, pranayama, pratyahara, and dharana. Only when our attention becomes unwavering, continuous, and unbroken, akin to the seamless flow of oil from one vessel to another, does the state of meditation grace us.

The most powerful tool we have for learning to live synchrodestiny, to see the connective patterns of the universe, to make miracles out of our desires, is meditation. Meditation allows us to place our attention and intention in these more subtle planes, giving us access to all that unseen, untapped information and energy.

— Deepak Chopra, *Synchrodestiny*

Understanding the Distinction Between Concentration and Meditation

Today, the term 'meditation' pervades our lives and is often used to describe a variety of techniques. It is vital to distinguish between concentration and meditation, as many practices are marketed as meditation. Meditation apps and YouTube videos often guide our attention, and while these are valuable tools for preparing the mind for meditation, it is essential to understand where they fit into the broader framework of practice.

Concentration involves periodic moments of focused attention on an object. The mind may wander to unrelated thoughts, and conscious effort is required to steer it back to the chosen object, such as the breath. This constitutes dharana practice.

3.2 Tatra pratyaya ekatanata dhyanam.

(In that dharana [tatra], when the causal possibilities [pratyayas] of experiences are all of the same kind [ekatanata], that is meditation [dhyanam].)

— Patanjali Yoga Sutras

In meditation, individual moments of concentration (dharana) coalesce into the seamless flow of dhyana, where attention flows to the object of focus effortlessly. And if our focus is the breath, we become profoundly absorbed in it and the experience becomes an intrinsic part of our consciousness and settles as a pratyaya (a possibility of experience). So even as we keep watching the breath, the underlying pratyayas, bubbling under the surface of consciousness, are all about the breath too. Thus, there is no need for effort to stay with the breath, as the attention flows continuously toward it (ekatanata).

Pratyahara, Dharana, Dhyana, and Samadhi—What's the Difference?

To clarify the subtle distinctions between pratyahara, dharana, dhyana, and samadhi, Manoj Kaimal draws an analogy using an archer.

In this analogy, the arrow symbolises our attention. Pratyahara equates to the archer pulling back the arrow, signifying the withdrawal of attention. Dharana corresponds to the archer fixing their gaze firmly on the target. This phase is quite challenging because numerous distractions surround the archer, demanding significant effort to maintain focus on the target.

Dhyana occurs when the practitioner experiences a state where effort becomes obsolete, and attention, like an arrow, flows seamlessly towards the target. In this phase, the practitioner enjoys and observes the arrow's flight toward the target, reflecting the meditative state.

Finally, the state of samadhi is reached when the arrow finds its mark, merging with the target. Here, the practitioner's attention and the object of attention become unified as one.

Sit Like Valmiki

A compelling story that highlights the essence of meditation involves the revered sage Valmiki, renowned as the Adi Kavi, or the first poet of Sanskrit literature. He is celebrated for his epic masterpiece, Ramayana, and is also credited with the authorship of the profound philosophical text, Yoga Vasishta.

It might intrigue you to learn that the great sage Valmiki, in his earlier life, was a highway robber, named Ratnakara. One providential encounter with sage Narada altered the course of his existence. Sage Narada posed a poignant question: Will Ratnakara's family, for whose sake he was committing these crimes, bear the burden of his sins? When Ratnakara sought his family's opinion, they unequivocally disassociated themselves from his misdeeds. This revelation shook him to his core, making him realise the sole responsibility he bore for his actions.

Ratnakara returned to sage Narada with a broken heart. Sage Narada, having sensed the great potential in Ratnakara, gave him the mantra 'Ma ra' and instructed him to chant it ceaselessly until his return. Ratnakara took these words literally, embarking on an unwavering meditation journey. He sat in a meditative posture for years, chanting the name of Rama without nourishment or sleep. Insects traversed his unmoving body, yet he remained steadfast. Many years passed, during which his form became concealed beneath a shroud of anthill. When sage Narada eventually returned, he unearthed Ratnakara from the anthill and bestowed him with the name Valmiki, symbolising his rebirth from this Valmika, or anthill.

The transformative power of meditation, represented by Ratnakara's profound commitment to dhyanam, was pivotal in his evolution into the sage Valmiki.

Manoj Kaimal frequently emphasises the lesson of 'Sitting like Sage Valmiki'. This metaphor encourages students to remain undisturbed by the crawling ants of restlessness, itchiness, and distraction that may encroach upon their bodies during meditation.

Fostering Inner Connection

Yoga, an ancient and comprehensive tradition encompassing practices like dhyanam, provides us with a profound approach to alleviate our suffering. The Yoga Sutras state, 'dukhameva sarvam vivekinah,' which implies that a discerning individual recognises life's inherent suffering, even if it may initially appear pleasurable. The essence of yogic practice revolves around the transformation and ultimate transcendence of this suffering.

The transformation begins by consciously diverting our attention from the captivating allure of the external world, which often lulls us into a nearly hypnotic trance, to the exploration of our inner world. Our connection with the outer world is primarily facilitated through our indriyas, the sensory organs—eyes, ears, nose, tongue, and skin. The sensory allure of the external world is likened to 'indriya jala', a net that ensnares our senses.

This shift in focus enables us to establish an inner connection. As we explore our true nature, we embark on the journey to live an authentic life. While the word 'alignment' in the realm of yoga might immediately evoke thoughts of foot placement, hip squareness, and arm positioning, the most profound alignment is observed in the way we lead our lives. It is the harmony between our intentions, words, and actions, between our inner and outer worlds.

The key to nurturing any relationship, be it with work, children, friends, or partners, lies in developing a deep interest. Where genuine interest exists, attention naturally follows, and any attempts to force interest are futile. The same principle applies to our inner world. As we cultivate curiosity and interest in its exploration, our inner landscape begins to illuminate. By grappling with questions, maintaining an open mind, exploring diverse philosophies and alternative perspectives, and delving into our life experiences, we traverse the path toward becoming more conscious, expansive human beings.

As we endeavour to work with our mind and consciously direct it toward states of ease and harmony, our body and breath emerge as our most potent allies. The revered sage Vyasa likens consciousness to a 'nadi' (river) that can flow in two directions—either toward 'kalyana' (auspiciousness) or 'papa' (inauspiciousness). Thus, we need to remain a 'sakshi' (a witness) maintaining objective awareness of our mind's state without succumbing to identification, judgement, or becoming entangled in its dramatic fluctuations. This allows us to cultivate 'viveka' (discriminative wisdom), which empowers us to make challenging choices and break free from the relentless grip of patterns that hinder our progress, steering us toward auspiciousness. Yoga practice embodies 'buddhi yuktah karma', actions guided by intellect, translating into conscious choices and skillful living.

The Answer

The practice of meditation bestows upon us an invaluable gift: it emancipates us from the grip of our often irritable, frustrated, desire-ridden, competitive, self-comparing, self-absorbed, and anxiety-prone selves with which we are deeply entwined. Each day, we find ourselves confronted by situations that trigger impulsive reactions from within us, causing us to respond without reflection or awareness. It's these everyday scenarios that highlight the necessity for regular practices that can help us regain our equilibrium and prevent us from falling apart at the seams.

Through our diligent meditation practice, we are offered fleeting glimpses of our limitless and expanded nature, each leaving an indelible mark on our subconscious mind. Over time, these imprints grow increasingly potent, such that they permeate our very essence. Impressions of tranquillity, unconditional love, interconnectedness, and joy become so deeply ingrained that they evolve into an inseparable part of our inherent character. It is then that we begin to sense the universal self, a transcendental presence that manifests as our complex individual self. This profound shift equips us with the ability to not just exist but to thrive, as we navigate life from an authentic, expansive, and elevated state of being.

In essence, meditation acts as a profound catalyst for the transformation of our inner landscape. It liberates us from our habitual, constricted responses to life's challenges and fosters an unwavering connection with the core of our being. This gradual process enables us to evolve into individuals who engage with the world from a place of profound authenticity, wisdom, and love.

* * *

Practical Exercises

❖ **Jyoti Mudra**

Jyoti Mudra is a profound practice that guides you toward inner illumination. Here is how to perform it:

- Begin by sitting comfortably in a cross-legged position, with your eyes gently closed and your spine erect.
- Spend a few minutes focusing on your breath to calm your mind and create a tranquil inner space.
- Using Ujjai breathing technique, inhale deeply and fill your lungs with air.
- At the end of your inhalation, gently press your eyeballs inward and upward using your index fingers. Keep your focus on the inner light that you perceive.
- You can also employ your other fingers to close off your senses. Use your thumbs to gently plug your ears, your middle fingers to lightly seal your nostrils, and your ring and little fingers to close your mouth. By doing this, you effectively shut out

the external world and direct the outward flowing energy of your senses, towards the inner light.

- Release your hold gently as you exhale.

To begin, perform three rounds of this practice and strive to prolong your focus on the inner light each time. This practice can lead to profound inner experiences.

❖ 7-Chakra Dhyana Meditation Based on Bija seed Mantra Chanting

This meditation practice, rooted in the power of bija (seed) mantras, is a potent method for elevating your mental and physical energies. It helps harmonise your mind and body while releasing any energetic blockages. Here is how you can engage in this practice:

- Begin by sitting comfortably in a cross-legged position, with your eyes gently closed and your spine upright.
- Note that the pronunciation of the bija mantras may be slightly different in different traditions; for example, 'Lam' may be vocalised as 'Langgggggg', 'Vam' as Vangggggg, etc.
- While chanting the bija mantras, you can further enhance your experience by lightly pressing your thumbs into your ear openings. This will allow you to feel the vibrations of the bija mantras more profoundly.

Now, let's explore each chakra in detail:

1. **Muladhara Chakra**

   - Direct your awareness to the root chakra situated at the base of the spine.

   - Observe the sensations in this area as you breathe in and out for 1-2 minutes.

   - The bija mantra for this chakra is 'Lam'. Inhale deeply, then audibly chant 'Lammmmm' as you exhale five times.

   - Continue to focus on the sensations at the Muladhara space as you mentally chant 'Lammmmm' with each exhalation for another minute. Let go of deliberate chanting and immerse yourself in the arising vibrations.

2. **Swadhisthana Chakra**

   - Shift your awareness to the pelvic region.

   - Pay attention to the sensations in this region as you breathe in and out for 1-2 minutes.

   - The bija mantra for the Swadhisthana chakra is 'Vam'. Inhale deeply and audibly chant 'Vammmmm' as you exhale, repeating this five times.

   - Keep your focus on the Swadhisthana space and the energy within as you mentally chant 'Vammmm' with each exhalation for one minute. Allow the vibration to fill your awareness.

3. **Manipura Chakra**
   - Bring your awareness to your navel area.
   - Spend 1-2 minutes observing the sensations as you breathe.
   - The bija mantra for the Manipura chakra is 'Ram'. Inhale deeply and audibly chant 'Rammmmm' as you exhale, repeating this five times.
   - Continue to focus on the Manipura space and the energy there while mentally chanting 'Rammmm' with each exhalation for one minute. Let the vibrations permeate your awareness.

4. **Anahata Chakra**
   - Shift your awareness to the heart centre.
   - Spend 1-2 minutes observing the sensations as you breathe.
   - The bija mantra for the Anahata chakra is 'Yam'. Inhale deeply and audibly chant 'Yammmmm' as you exhale, repeating this five times.
   - Maintain your focus on the Anahata space and the energy there as you mentally chant 'Yammmm' with each exhalation for one minute. Absorb the vibrations into your consciousness.

5. **Vishuddhi Chakra**
   - Direct your awareness to the throat area.
   - Spend 1-2 minutes observing the sensations as you breathe.
   - The bija mantra for the Vishuddhi chakra is 'Ham'. Inhale deeply and audibly chant 'Hammmmm' as you exhale, repeating this five times.
   - Keep your attention on the Vishuddhi space and the energy within as you mentally chant 'Hammmm' with each exhalation for one minute. Allow the vibrations to saturate your awareness.

6. **Ajna Chakra**
   - Focus on the third eye chakra, located just above the junction of your eyebrows.
   - Spend 1-2 minutes observing the sensations as you breathe.
   - The bija mantra for the Ajna chakra is 'Sham' (though 'Om' is also used). Inhale deeply and audibly chant 'Shammmmm' as you exhale, repeating this five times.
   - Maintain your awareness on the Ajna space and the energy within as you mentally chant 'Shammmm' with each exhalation for one minute. Allow the vibrations to permeate your consciousness.

7. Sahasrara Chakra

   - Direct your awareness to the crown chakra,
     Sahasrara, located at the top of your head.

   - Spend 2 minutes observing the sensations as
     you breathe.

   - The bija mantra for the Sahasrara chakra
     is 'Om'. Inhale deeply and audibly chant
     'Ommmmmm' as you exhale, repeating this
     five times.

   - Continue to focus on the space at the top of
     your head and the energy there as you mentally
     chant 'Ommmm' with each exhalation for one
     minute. Embrace the vibrations and allow
     them to infuse your consciousness.

Stay with the energy of the Sahasrara chakra. As
the channel of communication between the individual
and universal consciousness opens at the sahasrara, the
potent universal energy flows into the causal, subtle and
physical layers of the body, enabling you to manifest your
best self—physically, emotionally, and spiritually. Simply
BE.

Karpuramanale yadvat saindhavam salile yatha
Tatha sandhiyamanam ca manastattve viliyate.

(As camphor in fire and as salt in water, so does
the mind dissolve in the true state.)

—**Hathayogapradipika**

Chapter 10

SAMADHI

The concept of samadhi lies beyond the grasp of ordinary understanding and intellectual comprehension, making words and descriptions inadequate in capturing its true nature. In fact, it can only be fully comprehended through direct experience.

In the state of samadhi, the awareness and identity of the meditator, the process of meditation, and the object of meditation seamlessly merge into a singular entity. Moreover, there are also multiple levels of samadhi that one can progress through.

Patanjali's profound wisdom, as expounded in Yoga Sutra 3.3, invites us to explore the extraordinary realms of awareness and profound absorption within samadhi. And within the sacred realm of samadhi, Patanjali poetically expresses the concept of 'artha matra nirbhasam', which signifies a state where only the purest essence radiates, captivating our inner mental and intellectual faculties with its radiant luminosity.

3.3 Tadeva arthamatranirbhasam svarupasunyam iva samadhih.
(Samadhi is the state you progress to from meditation where there is the shining of the object alone, devoid of a separate subject.)

— Patanjali Yoga Sutras

Generally, our consciousness is entangled in preexisting patterns of ignorance known as avidya samskaras, which continuously generate states of suffering, known as dukha. Through our practice of dharana, where we consciously and deliberately direct our attention towards chosen objects of focus, we aim to reclaim control over our attention and liberate it from the tyranny of past conditioning (samskaras). Once we master this and concentration starts naturally flowing as dhyana, we reach the initial stage of samadhi, called samprajnata samadhi. In this state, wisdom (prajna) emerges, dispelling ignorance (avidya). Avidya involves misperceptions such as confusing the impermanent with the permanent, suffering with joy, or the non-self with the self. Samprajnata samadhi dismantles these false notions.

For instance, if you select the sensation of breath as your meditation object, dhyana signifies the effortless focus exclusively on the breath's sensations, excluding all other distractions. Samadhi occurs when the mere sensation of breath unveils spontaneous insights, such as the recognition of impermanence. With each inhale and exhale marking a beginning and an end, the practitioner becomes absorbed in the realisation that all living beings are impermanent. This insight liberates one from attachments to material things, leading to a state of liberation and heightened awareness. The four phases of liberation through insights are collectively referred to as samprajnata samadhi. It is important to note that all experiences, whether rooted in insight (vidya) or ignorance (avidya), are vrttis, or fluctuations of consciousness, which leave behind samskaras, or latent impressions.

As Patanjali asserts in 1.50, 'taj jah samskaro anya samskara pratibandhi', the practitioner's recurrent experiences of samadhi generate samadhi samskaras, which begin to counteract the influence of preexisting ignorant samskaras (avidya). As samadhi samskaras become increasingly predominant in the fertile soil of our consciousness, they gradually neutralise the effects of the existing samskaras of ignorance (avidya). The wisdom attained in the samprajnata samadhi experiences erases the imprints of previous samskaras, leaving behind only samskaras of wisdom.

Sage Vyasa elucidates samprajnata samadhi, also known as the samadhi of wisdom, as a state of complete absorption of consciousness with a chosen support, termed alambana. This state unfolds in four phases, progressing from gross (vitarka) to subtle (vichara), then to joy (ananda), and finally culminating in the experience of 'I-am-ness' (asmita). This progression resembles a filtering process that eliminates various layers of misidentifications from our intelligence.

To illustrate this concept, Manoj Kaimal, in his book, *Making Patanjali Palatable*, uses the analogy of installing a water filter in one's house to separate impurities and dirt from the water, leaving only pure water for consumption. Similarly, samprajnata samadhi gradually filters the gross elements, such as the body and mind, from consciousness through these four stages until one resides in the pure state of asmita.

He explains that individuals in this state of consciousness operate from unshakable peace, serenity, and wisdom, described in the Bhagavad Gita as 'sthita prajna', signifying stable wisdom. Samprajnata samadhi serves as a sanctuary of profound serenity, giving rise to love, joy, and liberating wisdom like divine nectar.

Moving forward, in the subsequent state of asamprajnata samadhi, Maharishi Patanjali explains that 'tasyapi nirodhe sarvanirodhat nirbijah samadhi'. Here, even the wisdom-related fluctuations and impressions (vrttis and samskaras) from samprajnata samadhi are negated. This leads to a complete dissolution of all substrates of individualised consciousness. While a wisdom-realised intellect has already dispelled delusion, a new identity may form around this wisdom, such as 'I, the wise one', 'I, the swamiji', or 'I, the saint'. In asamprajnata, the practitioner negates these self-identifications ('I am', or aham) with 'Not I' (naham). Consequently, there is a complete dissolution of the mind, intellect, and identity, allowing the practitioner to reside fully in their essential state. This state is beautifully expressed by Adi Shankara in his ecstatic composition, 'Nirvana Shatakam', wherein he sings, 'mano buddhi ahamkara chittani naham . . . sivoham sivoham', which translates to 'I am not the mind, intellect, ego—I am Shiva'.

In its essence, samadhi represents a state of pure and crystal-clear awareness that expands beyond our usual limited self into an extraordinary expanse. It harmoniously blends the abyss of shunya, signifying absolute emptiness, with the richness of purnam, symbolising absolute fullness, transcending the constraints of duality.

In this transcendent state, the familiar awareness of one's physical self dissolves, much like mist softly evaporating to reveal the radiant expanse of the cosmos. All external distractions, along with notions of place, direction, and time, fade into nothingness. Patanjali's term 'svarupa shunyam' captures the idea that all previously held identities become null and void in this state.

This profound state of samadhi is regarded as the pinnacle of yogic practice, where the seeker experiences union with the omnipresent and omniscient essence of the universe. It signifies an awakening to the boundless dimensions of the soul and stands as a testament to the profound depths of human consciousness.

* * *

Practical Exercise

❖ Outdoor 5-Elements Meditation

Find a comfortable seated position outdoors. Close your eyes and tune in to the energy around you. Take a moment to simply be present. Then, focus on your breath, feeling the inhale and exhale through your nostrils. As you do this, your mind will naturally settle.

Connect with the earth beneath you. Feel its stability and solid presence. Notice the earthy qualities within your body, particularly in your musculoskeletal system, which provides structure and support. Sense the earth within and around you.

Our planet's surface is primarily covered by water, with vast oceans, flowing rivers, and serene lakes. Visualise these bodies of water and hold onto that image. Recognise the water element within you. Every one of your seventy trillion cells contains a watery environment that keeps them together. Connect to the essence of water within yourself and in the world around you.

Now, feel the gentle warmth of the sun's rays on your skin. Connect with the pure sensation of warmth as it envelops your body. Recognise the fire element within you, manifesting as your digestive fire, which processes food and life experiences. Sense this internal fire and its essence.

Notice the air as it gracefully touches your skin, representing the element of air. In yogic philosophy, air is associated with the heart space. Bring your awareness to your heart and focus on love, which lies at the core of yoga philosophy. Reflect on the qualities of friendliness, goodwill, compassion, and equanimity. Feel these elevated emotions within your heart and extend them to the world around you.

Now, lie down and gaze at the expansive sky, contemplating the infinite space. Sense the vastness within your mind and realise that space is an integral part of you too. Whether you examine your bones, muscles, or atoms, you will find that they are predominantly composed of pure space. Embrace the boundless, indivisible, and limitless nature of space, both within and outside of yourself. Feel yourself as a continuum of the universal space, time and energy.

Epilogue

As we have discussed, the practice of yoga equips us with a set of tools encompassed within the various limbs of yoga—yamas, niyamas, asana, pranayama, and pratyahara—that prepare our bodies and minds to attain higher states of consciousness, namely dharana, dhyana, and samadhi.

These practices are not merely esoteric; they are practical and can be seamlessly integrated into our daily lives. For instance, when stress looms large due to impending deadlines and our bodies become tense, we can unroll our yoga mat near the computer and engage in deep stretches and heart-opening backbends to alleviate accumulated tension and unblock energy. In times of anxiety, while stuck in a traffic jam or before a medical procedure, we can employ conscious deep breathing or other techniques that activate the relaxation response. When we have invested significant time and effort in a project and await a decision, we can surrender the outcome and take solace in ishwara pranidhana.

Furthermore, our personal growth and transformation ripple outward, influencing the lives of those around us, including family, friends, colleagues, and co-workers, as we share the gifts of the practice. The impact of our actions today extends beyond our immediate circumstances; it leaves a lasting legacy that touches the lives of future generations as well.

Many of my students have discovered profound benefits from yoga in coping with depression, anxiety, panic attacks, mood swings, irritability, and the feelings of helplessness and hopelessness, especially in their battles against cancer and on their paths to recovery. They have even enrolled their young children as my students, ensuring that the next generation grows up with an awareness of the significance of mind-body-breath techniques. This way, regardless of where life may take them and the challenges they may face, they possess the empowering tools of yoga.

Both of my sons are practitioners of yoga, and as a mother, nothing brings me greater satisfaction than knowing they have embraced the philosophy and practices of yoga. These tools offer them a softer and more elevated perspective, helping them navigate life's twists and turns. As much as we love and protect our children, they have to face life independently, and it is the wisdom of yoga philosophy, which connects them to their inner self, that provides a guiding light in any situation.

In essence, yoga serves as the original 'self-help' tool, illuminating the path to self-discovery and transformation. May the light of yoga shine brightly in our hearts and inspire those around us to embark on their own journeys. To conclude this book, I offer a verse from the Bhagavad Gita that inspires me and is a clarion call to 'Lift Yourself by Yourself'. It is my hope that this message will serve as an inspiration to all of you as well.

6.5 Uddhared atmanatmanam natmanam avasadayet
Atmaiva hyatmano bandhur atmaiva ripur atmanah.
(Elevate yourself through the power of your mind, and not degrade yourself. For the mind can be a friend and also the enemy of the self.)

— The Bhagavad Gita

ACKNOWLEDGEMENTS

This book would not have been possible without the support and blessings of so many wonderful people. I truly feel the grace of the universe flowing towards me through their presence in my life. The list is surely incomplete but my deepest gratitude to:

R. Madhavan for graciously lending his name in support of the book and the greater cause of sharing the wisdom of yoga to the modern seeker as well as to Vikram Kumar for making it happen.

K. K Shailaja for being an inspiration to women and supporting the book with her valuable insights and my dear friends Padmaja and Vinod for being a part of this book's journey.

His Excellency, B. N. Reddy, for having released my first book *Yoga Shakti* in Malaysia and for supporting this second one with his words of encouragement.

Yogacharya Dr Ananda Balayogi Bhavanani whose selfless sharing and passionate in-depth teaching inspires me on my own yoga path. Dr Ananda's teachings were a beacon of light during the dark covid times and are reflected in this book.

Dr Vasant Lad, Dr Robert Svoboda, Dr Shirley Telles, Dr Prasad Kaipa, Dr Vikrant Singh Tomar, and Dr Kausthub Desikachar, all luminaries and trailblazers in their respective fields of Ayurveda, Yoga and Vedanta, for taking the time from their very busy lives to endorse my book.

Ramkumar who unhesitatingly and ever-so-generously goes the extra mile to support the book and the cause of yoga.

Mataji Divyananda who will always have a special place in my life for having inspired me on the path of yoga 24 years ago with her radiant personality and presence.

Manoj Kaimal, my teacher, Guru Manasa Yoga, for having shaped my perspective on yoga with his focus on the mind. His unique philosophy-based experiential asana classes over these last 20 years have enriched my life and inspired me to share his teachings which form the bedrock of this book.

My students at 'Mat and Beyond Yoga' in Malaysia, the U.K., and the U.S.A. who resonate with my teachings.

My family and friends in Malaysia, the US, and India. My mother Sushila Jayakumaran, who loves me best, my uncle M. K. Vijayashanker, and my aunts Chandrika Vijayashanker and Indira Prabhakaran who are my personal cheerleading squad. Mini Padmam, who is always there for me.

My husband, Prem, and my precious sons, Vyshnav and Krishan, for the stability and joy they bring to my life.

My publishers, Hay House India, for their faith in the book.

To the universe which shapes and designs my life with passion, meaning, and purpose.

References

Books

1. Bhavanani, Ananda. 2011. *Understanding the Yoga Darshan: An Exploration of the Yoga Sutra of Maharishi Patanjali.* Dhivyananda Creations. Puducherry.

2. Bhavanani, Ananda. 2013. *Yoga Chikitsa: The Application of Yoga as a Therapy.* Dhivyananda Creations. Puducherry.

3. Bhavanani, Ananda. 2017. *A Primer of Yoga Theory.* Dhivyananda Creations. Puducherry.

4. Iyengar, B. K. S. 2008. *Light on the Yoga Sutras of Patanjali.* HarperCollins Publishers.

5. Manoj Kaimal. 2008. *Making Patanjali Palatable.*

6. Chopra, Deepak. 2003. *Synchrodestiny.* Rider

7. Chopra, Deepak. 2013. *Super Brain.* Rider.

8. Chopra, Deepak. 2015. *Super Genes.* Harmony. New York.

9. Desikachar, T. K. V. 1995. *The Heart of Yoga.* Inner Traditions India. Vermont.

10. Goleman, Daniel and Davidson, Richard J. 2017. *The Science of Mediation*. Penguin Life.

11. Iyengar, B. K. S., Evans, John J. & Abrams, Douglas. 2005. *Light on Life*. Rodale International. London.

12. Kaimal, Manoj. 2007. *Celebration of Asanas*.

13. Nestor, James. 2020. *Breath*. Riverhead Books. New York.

14. Parthasarathy, A. 2001. *Choice Upanishads*. A. Parthasarathy. Mumbai.

15. Satchidananda. 1978. *The Yoga Sutras of Patanjali*. Integral Yoga Publications. Virginia.

16. Sivananda, Swami. 2008. *Mind: Its Mysteries and Control*. The Divine Life Society. Shivanandanagar.

Articles

1. Buric I, Farias M, Jong J, Mee C & Brazil IA. 2017 What Is the Molecular Signature of Mind–Body Interventions? A Systematic Review of Gene Expression Changes Induced by Meditation and Related Practices. Frontiers in Immunology, 8(670).

2. Cromie, William J. 2002. Meditation changes temperatures. Published in Harvard Gazette. Link: https://news.harvard.edu/gazette/story/2002/04/meditation-changes-temperatures/.

3. Kestel, Dévora. 2022. The State of Mental Health Globally in the Wake of the COVID-19 Pandemic

and Progress on the WHO Special Initiative for Mental Health (2019-2023). Published online at UN Chronicle. Link: https://www.un.org/en/un-chronicle/state-mental-health-globally-wake-covid-19-pandemic-and-progress-who-special-initiative.

4. Ornish D, Lin J, Chan JM, Epel E, Kemp C, Weidner G, Marlin R, Frenda SJ, Magbanua MJM, Daubenmier J, Estay I, Hills NK, Chainani-Wu N, Carroll PR, Blackburn EH. 2013. Effect of comprehensive lifestyle changes on telomerase activity and telomere length in men with biopsy-proven low-risk prostate cancer: 5-year follow-up of a descriptive pilot study. Lancet Oncol, 14(11), pp. 1112-1120.

5. Shulte, B. 2015. 'Harvard neuroscientist: Meditation not only reduces stress, here's how it changes your brain', The Washington Post, 26 May 2015.

6. Schutte, Nicola S., J Malouff, John M. & Keng, Shian-Ling. 2020. Meditation and telomere length: a meta-analysis, Psychology & Health, 35(8), pp. 901-915.

7. Walton, Alice G. 2017. 'How Meditation and Yoga Can Alter The Expression Of Our Genes', Forbes, 19 June 2017.

CONNECT WITH
HAY HOUSE
ONLINE

 hayhouse.co.in   **f** @hayhouseindia

 @hayhouseindia   **X** @hayhouseindia

Join the conversation about latest products, events,
exclusive offers, contests, giveaways and more.

'*The gateways to wisdom and knowledge
are always open.*'

Louise Hay

Milton Keynes UK
Ingram Content Group UK Ltd.
UKHW020752240724
446081UK00001B/77

9 788119 554515